MINOR UPA

With Original Text, Introduction, English Rendering, and Comments

SWAMI MADHAVANANDA

𝓐dvaita Ashrama
(Publication Department)
5 Dehi Entally Road
Kolkata 700 014

Published by
Swami Mumukshananda
President, Advaita Ashrama
Mayavati, Champawat, Himalayas
from its Publication Department, Kolkata
Email : advaita@vsnl.com
Website : www.advaitaonline.com

ISBN 81-7505-104-3

Printed in India at
Gipidi Box Co.
Kolkata 700 014

CONTENTS

CONTENTS

INTRODUCTION

Upanishads which form a portion of the Vedas contain the records of spiritual truths, the eternal teachings of religion. These truths were discovered by different persons at different times and handed down to posterity. As time went on, these truths which were first handed down orally were recorded in writing in book form. They treat of various topics which are not quite systematised for they have been merely jotted down without any attempt at arrangement. The ideas are wonderful and are always progressive taking one to higher and higher stages of spiritual realisation. We get, as it were, an insight into the mind of the sages from them. The thoughts at first were undeveloped but gradually became finer and finer. The Aryans in their attempts to find a solution of the great problems of life and death in the external world failed and came to the conclusion that the senses could not help them much in that direction. We find utterances in the Upanishads which declare the utter inability of the senses to reach the ultimate reality. They therefore left the external world and fell back upon the internal one. They took up the study of the Ātman, which finally gave them the solution they sought. The Upanishads present to us the Sublime in the most exquisite poetry in the whole world of literature, which takes us away from the world of senses to a region far beyond their reach. We get a glimpse of the Absolute, which we cannot

grasp with our senses but yet feel certain. It is न तत्र सूर्यो
भाति न चन्द्रतारकं नेमा विद्युतो भान्ति कुतोऽयमग्निः—'There the sun
cannot illumine nor the moon nor the stars, the flash of
lightning cannot illumine the place what to speak of this
mortal fire.' The language, however, is direct, and there
is no mistaking in its meaning.

Their Place in Vedic Literature

The Upanishads generally form a part of the
Āranyakas which are themselves a part of the Brāhmana
portion of the Vedas. But though this is the place
generally allotted to them, yet they are not always written
after the ritualistic portion of the Vedas for we do find
that many of them form a part of the Samhitā and
Brāhmana portions of the Vedas, as for example the Isha
and Kena Upanishads. Some of the Upanishads are,
however, independent, not being comprised in any of the
Brāhmanas or other parts of the Vedas. This and the fact
that some of the Upanishadic doctrines were taught by
the Kshatriyas have led many scholars to arrive at a rather
hasty conclusion that the Upansihadic doctrines orig-
inated among the Kshatriyas independent of the
Brāhmanas and Āranyakas which formed the sacred lore
of the Brahmins. Though the Kshatriyas are respsonsible
for many an Upanishadic doctrine yet from the Upanishads themselves we get ample evidence of the fact that
the natural order was for the Brahmins to teach the Ātma-
jnāna—the knowledge of the Self to the other castes.
During the age of the Upanishads a more rational inquiry
with regard to God, Soul, and Nature engaged the best
minds; the ritualistic and sacrificial worship failed to give

any satisfaction to them. The fact that even the Kshatriyas took keen interest in philosophic speculations is only an evidence of this fact, and for the matter of that even women took great interest in such speculations in that age. Knowledge was welcome from all sources irrespective of caste or creed. The fame of a great sage like Yājnavalkya or a king like Ajātashatru would spread far and wide, and students of all castes from all parts of India would flock to them to learn what they had to teach. Such was the keen quest after knowledge of the age. That some of the Upanishads are independent, not being comprised in any of the Brāhmanas or other parts of the Vedas, can be explained if we remember that much of the Vedic literature is now extinct, and these Upanishads might have formed parts of the extinct Brāhmanas. There were also as many as 1180 Shākhās of Vedic literature, and each school is said to have had one Upanishad attached to its Shākhā. Most of these Shākhās are now no more. The Upanishads are also known as the Jnānakānda or knowledge-portion as opposed to the ritualistic portion of the Vedas which is known as the Karmakānda or work-portion. They are also known as the Vedanta — the end of the Vedas, as they generally form the last portion of the Vedas and also as they contain the highest purpose of the Vedas — the last word of the Vedas with respect to that supreme knowledge which frees the individual from bondage.

Meaning of the Word 'Upanishad'

The word Upanishad has been derived variously by various scholars and Bhāshyakāras. 'The Western scholars', says Prof.Max Müller, 'are agreed in deriving

Upa-ni-shad from the root *sad* to sit down, preceded by the two prepositions, *ni*, down, and *upa*, near, so that it expresses the idea of session, an assembly of pupils sitting down near their teacher to listen to his instructions.' He himself also holds this view though he admits the word never occurs in this sense anywhere. The commentators of the East, however, derive it from the root *sad* in the sense of destruction or approaching, which gives the word Upanishad the meaning, that which destroys ignorance, the cause of Samsāra, by revealing the knowledge of the supreme Self and hence knowledge, and secondly that which helps us to approach or attain Brahman. We shall, however, be justified by the Upanishads themselves if we give the word the meaning, secret doctrine or knowledge derived from such doctrine. That this knowledge was imparted in secret, only to the deserving and concealed from the unfit, there is ample proof. 'This highest mystery in the Vedanta should not be given to one whose passions have not been subdued, nor to one who is not a son or who is not a pupil' (Shvet.Up.VI.22). Also in Maitr. Up. VI .29 the same idea occurs, and in addition we have: 'To him alone who is devoted to his teacher only and endowed with all necessary qualities may he communicate it.' It was imparted only to earnest enquirers who were possessed of self-restraint and high moral discipline; to people who were free from desires for enjoyments as are attainable by the performances of sacrifices. Such alone, according to Shankara, were fit for an enquiry into Brhaman. Such an aspirant must possess the preliminary moral discipline called the Sādhana-chatushtaya according to Shankara. This consists (1) in the possession of the six ethical qualities, *shama*, *dama*, *titikshā*, *uparati*, *samādhāna*, and *shraddhā*, (2) in the renouncing of the desire for enjoyments of this life and heaven after death, (3) in the discrimination between the real and the unreal, and (4) in the desire for salvation.

It may be questioned why this discipline is necessary. The answer is that religion is not attained through mere book learning. Truth is far from mere intellectualism — the bane of this age, often leading to selfishness. It is purity of the heart that takes one to the highest. This discipline divests the mind of all its impurities and irrational bias and frees it from desires and attachments. When the mind attains this state of purity and steadiness, the Atman manifests Itself in Its native glory, तदा द्रष्टुः स्वरूपेऽवस्थानम्—'At that time the seer rests in his own state.' Hence the need of the preparatory discipline and the secrecy in imparting the knowledge, which, however, was not withheld from the really deserving and fit. It is this secrecy that has come to give the word Upanishad the meaning 'Secret doctrine' or 'Knowledge'.

The Number and Date of the Upanishads

There are about 108 Upanishads according to the Muktikopanishad and the Mahāvākyaratnāvali; but many more have been added to this number. Though some of them are evidently of a much later date and spurious, yet as a rule it is hard to fix their dates with certainty. This much can be said that a majority of those which are genuine are *much* older than the Buddhistic movement. The mere fact that some of the Upanishads, especially the minor ones, contain allusions to later dates, does not prove the later origin of these Upanishads, as in Sanskrit literature the substance of a book though of a very ancient date often receives a coating of later events in the hands of sectarians, in order to exalt their particular sects. Among these Upanishads those which on the face of them bear the evidence of genuineness and have been commented upon by the great Āchāryas or quoted by them as authorities in their commentaries may be taken as the oldest.

The Fundamental Doctrine of the Upanishads

What do these Upanishads teach? A cursory glance through them convinces one that they do not contain a systematised philosophical exposition. It is not possible to combine all the doctrines therein into one complete system without doing violence to many a text which would not fall in with the system. They are the repository of various thoughts and ideals that have since been worked out in detail by the Hindus. In them we find the germs of all subsequent development of the Indian religious thought. These Upanishads have been variously explained and in trying to elucidate a systematic philosophy out of these diverse texts commentators have often tortured texts to suit their own purpose. In the midst of all these varying methods of reading and commenting, it is very difficult to find the thread that runs through all of them. 'We, however, feel that there must be some common grounds for this apparently hopeless mass of confusion. In fact these texts are not at all anomalous but wonderfully harmonious, one idea leading up to the other. All the Upanishads generally begin with dualistic ideas of worship and end with a grand flourish of Advaitic ideas. The old idea of Arundhati-Nyāya applies here.

God is at first the Creator, Preserver, and Destroyer; then He is God immanent in nature; and at last we are taught that whatever is real is He. "Thou art that".'

The Upanishads have therefore finally one subject matter — the identity of the individual and the Supreme Self — ब्रह्मात्मैक्य-साक्षात्कार-विषयः। The discovery of that by knowing which everything is known is their one theme. To find unity in the varieties in the world is their one object. They claim that it is One Being that is manifesting Itself in all these various forms and that this Self alone is real. This the Upanishads, however, do not establish by any elaborate philosophical discussions or analysis of the mind, but it is just put there as a result of direct perception; and the conviction with which it is uttered cannot come from anything short of such direct perception. This is the reason why Vedanta is generally associated with Advaita; and the interpretation given by Shankara and his system of thought is called the Vedanta system or Vedanta *par excellence*, though as a matter of fact there are many other systems, which reasonably lay claim to this title — for they too base their systems on the Upanishads. Shankara's interpretation, however, comes nearer to the spirit of the Upanishads and hence his better claim. The commentators are all more or less guilty of text-torturing. That was partly due to the fact that the Shruti was held supreme and beyond reason, reason being given only a subordinate place. 'It was not for a commentator, however great, to say anything regarding the Shruti on his own authority based on reason or experience; he could only interpret the Shruti.' He had no more freedom, and hence he often twisted texts to squeeze his own meaning out of them.

The Phenomenal World

Though the sages of the Upanishads were firm in declaring that the Brahman alone was true, yet this world of duality which is a matter of experience to everyone had to be explained. They had to recognise this fact and had to harmonise this world with the one Reality, the Brahman. This they attempted by saying that this world is created out of Brahman; in It it exists, and in It is it dissolved at the end. In other words, Brahman is the essence of this world. This explanation, however, was perfected by Shankara by propounding what is known as the Vivarta-vāda or apparent manifestation of the world, giving the world a relative reality; and he is justified in this explanation by the Upanishads which often speak of the unreality and illusory character of the phenomenal world. In Sarvopanishad we have a concise explanation of Māyā and Vivarta-vāda. Vivarta-vāda is undoubtedly the most cogent explanation of creation.

According to Shankara, God is the material cause of the universe but only apparently and not in reality. The whole universe, as it exists, is that Being; yet It is unchaged; and all the changes are caused by Nāma and Rupa (name and form) which are the cause of all differentiation. When one is in ignorance one sees the phenomena and not the reality; when one realises the noumenon one does not see the phenomena. It is either the snake or the rope but never both simultaneously. Ignorance or Māyā is the cause of all this duality, the Absolute being mistaken for the world. 'This Māyā is not absolutely nothing or non-existent; for if it were, it could never produce the phenomena. It is not also existent, because that can be truly said only of the Absolute. So it is something which is neither; and in Vedanta it is called Anirvachaniya or inexpressible. This Māyā gives the name and form to what Brahman gives the material, and the latter seems transformed into all this.' There is no place in reality for the individual soul. The reality is one Existence, Sat, and the duality is due to ignorance. All our ideas of fear, misery, and other evils are false and due to the idea of differentiation and vanish with the knowledge of the Brahman or Self. 'Where one hears another, one sees another, that is small; where one does not see another, where one does not hear another that is the greatest, that is God. In that greatest is perfect happiness. In small things there is no happiness.'

Freedom

The attainment of this infiniteness is the liberation or Freedom — so the Upanishads preach. It is realised when man feels his own nature and the veil of ignorance drops away. This freedom or Mukti is our true nature. We are already that, and we have not to attain it; only we have to know this truth which is now covered by Māyā. 'If a man lives after this to work out his Karma which might have already taken effect, he lives as a Jivanmukta, gathering no fresh Karma. He has realised the mirage of the universe and is no longer deluded by it. The world has vanished for him. It may come back again, but no more as the same world of misery. The prison of misery has changed into Sat, Chit, Ānanda — Existence, Knowledge and Bliss Absolute.'

The study of the Upanishads : its benefits

The Upanishads are a mine of strength. They ask man not to be weak and grow moody over his weakness. While recognising human weaknesses, the Upanishads declare that sin can never cure sin. As one thinks so one becomes. If a man therefore thinks himself a sinner, a sinner he would be; but if he thinks himself strong and free, free he would become that moment. 'Abhih' (fearlessness) is the watchword of the Upanishads. 'They call on the weak, the miserable, and the downtrodden of all races, all creeds, and sects to stand on their feet, to have faith in themselves and be free, physically, mentally, and spiritually — for the infinite, all-powerful Atman is their true nature.' To the Hindu race which is now stranded and weak and divided into a thousand factions, there can be nothing more beneficial than the study of the Upanishads which speak of nothing but strength and solidarity of the universe. It may probably come as a keen surprise to the orthodox and bigoted that their conduct has not always been justifiable by their own scriptures, the Upanishads. To our westernised countrymen also, it will be a surprise to find such a mine of knowledge at home in their own scriptures while they have been going all the world over in search of that knowledge. To the Hindu in general, it would bring fresh vigour and life in his dead bones.

These Upanishads, though called minor in order to distinguish them from the ten well-known ones commented on by Shankarāchārya, are nonetheless very valuable. Of them, the Paramahamsopanishad belongs to the Sukla-Yajur-Veda, while all others are included in the Atharva-Veda.

MINOR UPANISHADS

PARAMAHAMSOPANISHAD

This Upanishad elaborately portrays the characteristic marks and ideals of the knower of Truth when he reaches the highest stage of life. It also speaks of the duties of those Sannyāsins who are on the way to knowledge.

Every Upanishad begins and ends with a Shānti-pātha or invocation of Peace, or an expiatory prayer to the Deities for the purpose of averting all evil and being in peace with the universe, which alone is conducive to perfect calmness and concentration of the mind needed for the study of such a subtle subject as the Self. So let us repeat:

ॐ भद्रं कर्णेभिः श्रृणुयाम देवा भद्रं पश्येमाक्ष-
भिर्यजत्राः । स्थिरैरङ्गैस्तुष्टुवांसस्तनूभिर्व्यशेम देवहितं
यदायुः । स्वस्ति न इन्द्रो वृद्धश्रवाः स्वस्ति नः पूषा
विश्ववेदाः । स्वस्ति नस्ताक्ष्योॅरिष्टनेमिः स्वस्ति नो
बृहस्पतिर्दधातु । ॐ शान्तिः शान्तिः शान्तिः ।
हरिः ॐ ॥

Om ! O Devas, may we hear with our ears what is auspicious ; may we see with our eyes what is auspicious, O ye worthy of worship ! May we enjoy the term of life allotted by the Devas, praising them with our body and limbs steady ! May the glorious Indra bless us ! May the all-knowing Sun bless us ! May Garuda, the

thunderbolt for evil, bless us ! May Brihaspati grant us
well-being ! Om ! Peace ! Peace ! Peace ! Hari Om !

अथ योगिनां परमहंसानां कोऽयं मार्गस्तेषां का
स्थितिरिति नारदो भगवन्तमुपगत्योवाच । तं भगवानाह ।
योऽयं परमहंसमार्गो लोके दुर्लभतरो न तु बाहुल्यो
यद्येको भवति स एव नित्यपूतस्थः स एव वेदपुरुष इति
विदुषो मन्यन्ते महापुरुषो यच्चित्तं तत्सर्वदा मय्येवाव-
तिष्ठते तस्मादहं च तस्मिन्नेवावस्थीयते । असौ स्वपुत्रमित्र-
कलत्रबन्ध्वादीञ्शिखायज्ञोपवीते स्वाध्यायं च सर्वकर्माणि
संन्यस्यायं ब्रह्माण्डं च हित्वा कौपीनं दण्डमाच्छादनं च
स्वशरीरोपभोगार्थाय च लोकस्योपकारार्थाय च परिग्रहेत्तच्च
न मुख्योऽस्ति कोऽयं मुख्य इति चेदयं मुख्यः ॥१॥

1. "What is the path of the Paramahamsa Yogis,[1]
and what are their duties ?"—was the question Nārada
asked on approaching the Lord Brahmā (the Creator).
To him the Lord replied : The path of the Paramahamsas
that you ask of is accessible[2] with the greatest difficulty
by people ; they have not many exponents, and it is enough
if there be one such.[3] Verily, such a one rests[4] in the ever-
pure Brahman ; he is verily the Brahman inculcated in the
Vedas—this is what the knowers of Truth hold ; he is the
great one,[5] for he rests his whole mind always in Me;[6]
and I, too, for that reason, reside[7] in him. Having[8]
renounced   his sons, friends, wife, and relations, etc.,[9]
and having done away with the Shikhā,[10] the holy thread,[11]
the study[12] of the Vedas, and all works,[13] as well as this
universe,[14] he should use[15] the Kaupina,[16] the staff, and just
enough clothes, etc.,[17] for the bare maintenance of his body,

and for the good[18] of all.   And that is not final.[19] If it is asked what this final is, it is as follows :

1   *Paramahamsa Yogis*—The Yogis are those who have controlled all the outgoing faculties of the mind and attained concentration by the practice of the eightfold means of Yoga, viz—Yama, Niyama, Asana, Prānāyāma, Pratyāhāra, Dhāranā, Dhyāna, and Samādhi. The Paramahamsas are those who have attained the superconscious state in which all illusion of the world has vanished in the direct realisation of Truth, the Oneness of existence. They belong to the highest order of Sannyāsins. The word is put here to qualify Yogis because they are sometimes seen to apply their powers or Siddhis to worldly ends, which brings on their downfall.   The Paramahamsas, however, having realised the hollowness of all earthly vanities through Knowledge renounce them.

2   *Is accessible etc.*—because this Paramahamsa path called Turiyā-shrama (the fourth order) is reached through the merits acquired by the strenuous exertions of many previous births.

3   *One such*—at any time in any country.

4   *Rests etc.*—is firmly established in the consciousness of "I am the Brahman".

5   *The great one*—not conditioned by anything, though living in the body.

6   *Me*—the Paramātman.

7   *Reside etc.*—In My own essence, there being no distinction between him and Me ; but not in those devoid of knowledge.

8   *Having etc.*—with a view to attaining the perfect and undis-turbed peace of mind, without having anything to identify his self with.

9   *Etc.*—implies servants, cattle, home, and fields—indeed all worldly possessions.

10   *Shikhā*—the tuft of hair on the crown of the head.

11   *The holy thread*—which marks one as belonging to the Three Varnas, and entitled to the performance of Vedic rites.

12   *Study etc.*—which is useful only so long as Truth is not realised. Mark, it is only the Veda, of all the scriptures of the world, which calls upon its believers to go beyond it.

13   *All works*—such as secular, Vaidika, obligatory, cere-monial, forbidden and those performed with a motive to gain prosperity either here or hereafter.

14 *This universe*—which by its various threads of desire binds the soul and charms it by its endless deceitful sports of Māyā.

15 *Use*—accept, but not with the idea, "These are *mine*."

16 *Kaupina etc.*—the Kaupina, for decency's sake; the Danda or staff, to ward off wild cows, snakes, and the like; clothes, just to protect himself from heat and cold.

17 *Etc.*—implies shoes, to protect the feet ·from the thorns or to avoid directly touching unclean spots.

18 *For the good etc.*—Though he does not care for those things for himself yet he may use them for the good of those who are devoted to their Svadharma, who by seeing the outward signs of the Danda etc. will recognise him as a Sannyāsin, and approaching him with reverence, will earn religious merit, by the gift of Bhikshā (food) (i.e. by the cultivation of the faculty of charity), and dispel their Ajnāna (nescience) by hearing his words of wisdom.

19 *Final*—Using those things are not, however, for the Paramahamsa of the highest stage.

न दण्डं न शिखां न यज्ञोपवीतं न चाच्छादनं चरति परमहंसः । न शीतं न चोष्णं न सुखं न दुःखं न मानावमाने च षड्रूमिवर्जं निन्दागर्वमत्सरदम्भदर्पेच्छाद्वेष-सुखदुःखकामक्रोधलोभमोहहर्षासूयाहंकारादींश्च हित्वा स्ववपुः कुणपमिव दृश्यते यतस्तद्धपुरपध्वस्तं संशय-विपरीतमिथ्याज्ञानानां यो हेतुस्तेन नित्यनिवृत्तस्तन्नित्य-बोधस्तत्स्वयमेवावस्थितिस्तं शान्तमचलमद्वयानन्दविज्ञान-घन एवास्मि । तदेव मम परमधाम तदेव शिखा च तदेवोप-वीतं च । परमात्मात्मनोरकत्वज्ञानेन तयोर्भेद एव विभग्नः सा संध्या ॥२॥

2. The Paramahamsa carries neither the staff, nor the hair-tuft, nor the holy thread nor any covering. He feels[1] neither cold, nor heat, neither happiness nor misery, neither honour, nor contempt etc.[2] It is meet that he should be beyond the reach of the six billows[3] of this world-ocean.

Having given up all thought of calumny,[4] conceit, jealousy, ostentation,[5] arrogance, attachment or antipathy to objects, joy and sorrow, lust, anger, covetousness, self-delusion, elation, envy, egoism[6], and the like,[7] he regards[8] his body as a corpse, as he has thoroughly destroyed the body-idea. Being eternally[9] free from the cause[10] of doubt,[11] and of misconceived[12] and false knowledge,[13] realising the Eternal Brahman, he lives in That himself, with the consciousness "I myself am He, I am That which is ever calm, immutable, undivided,[14] of the essence of knowledge-bliss, That alone is my real nature." That[15] (Jnāna) alone is his Shikhā. That (Jnāna) alone is his holy thread. Through the knowledge of the unity of the Jivātman with the Paramātman, the distinction between them is wholly gone too. This (unification) is his Sandhyā ceremony.

1 *He feels etc.*—Why he stands in no need of carrying the Danda etc. is told in this sentence. He being a Yogi rests absorbed in the Paramātman and has no consciousness of heat and cold, like a child absorbed in play, and because of his seeing no other self but his own in all, does not feel elated by honour paid to him, nor grieved by being disrespectfully treated.

2 *Etc.*—Implies all the dual throngs.

3 *Six billows*—hunger, thirst, grief, delusion, decay (by bodily disease), and death. Of these, the first two belong to the Prāna, the next two to the mind, and the last two to the body. It is but natural that the Yogi should not be affected by these changes as his aim is the knowledge of the Ātman which is bereft of all qualities.

4 *Calumny*—from others.

5 *Ostentation*—display of one's own spiritual practices before others to please them, or to gain name and fame.

6 *Egoism*—thinking the aggregate of the body, the senses etc. as the Self.

7 *The like*—such as the idea of mine-ness in objects of enjoyment.

8 *Regards etc.*—because of the absence of the idea of egoism in it. Just as men for fear of pollution by touching a corpse look at it from a distance, so the Yogi for fear of having the error of self-identity with the body again aroused, looks upon it as a mass of inert matter only, quite distinct from the Self.

9 *Eternally*—negates the reappearance of Avidyā once it is destroyed by knowledge of the Ātman.

10 *Cause etc.*—is Nescience, Avidyā, with everything connected with it, such as desire, attachment etc.

11 *Doubt*—as whether a thing seen in a mist is a stump or a man : as whether the Ātman is the doer and enjoyer or not.

12 *Misconceived knowledge*—as mistaking the mother-of-pearl for silver : as mistaking the body and the aggregate of the senses as the Ātman.

13 *False knowledge*—as believing the Ātman to be the doer and enjoyer. Doubt and misconceived knowledge also come under this category.

14 *Undivided*—being devoid of dual perception, as that of good and evil, which does not exist in the Ātman.

15 *That (Jñāna) etc.*—Though such a Paramahamsa has no outward signs of a Brāhmana, as the Shikhā and the holy thread, and does not perform any Sandhyā according to Vedic injunctions, yet he is to be regarded as higher than a Brāhmana, for he performs, by night and day, the true import of the Sandhyā—the union of the individual soul with the Supreme Soul.

सर्वान्कामान्परित्यज्य अद्वैते परमस्थितिः ।
ज्ञानदण्डो धृतो येन एकदण्डी स उच्यते ॥
काष्ठदण्डो धृतो येन सर्वाशी ज्ञानवर्जितः ।
स याति नरकान्घोरान्महारौरवसंज्ञकान् ॥
इदमन्तरं ज्ञात्वा स परमहंसः ॥३॥

3. He who relinquishing all desires[1] has his supreme rest[2] in the One without a second, and who holds the staff[3] of knowledge,[4] is the true Ekadandi. He[5] who carries a mere wooden staff, who takes to all sorts of sense-objects, and is devoid of Jnāna, goes to horrible hells[6] known as the Mahārauravas. Knowing[7] the distinction between these two, he becomes a Paramahamsa.

1 *All desires*—of enjoying the objects of the senses, here and hereafter, as they only taint the mind-stuff and bring on misery and bondage in the end.

2 *Rest etc.*—i.e. rests in the essence of pure bliss without knowing any break.

3 *Staff*—Danda ; generally, it is a symbol of authority and punishment. It is given to a twice-born man at the time of investi- ture with the sacred thread, signifying his admission into the Brahma- chāri (student) life. It is also received from the hands of the Guru at the time of one's taking Sannyāsa, not only to ward off physical dangers, but as a symbol to constantly remind the bearer of the great duties and responsibilities of his exalted position. Among the various orders of Sannyāsins there are Tridandis and Ekadandis ; the former carry in the right hand three long staves tied together so as to form one. The three staves are meant to represent Vāg-danda or control of speech, Kāya-danda or control of (bodily) desires, and Mano-danda or control of mind by Prānāyāma.

4 *Staff of knowledge*—The one staff of the Ekadandi represents Jnāna or the consciousness of "I am Brahman", and it is conceived as a Danda because it kills the deadly animals of attachment, hate etc., which are the offspring of duality or diversity.

5 *He*—who is Paramahamsa in name only.

6 *Hells*—i.e., experiences various states of awful pain and misery in the after-life for his having been false to the ideals of the Order, his Svadharma.

7 *Knowing etc.*—Knowing the vast difference between the Pravritti and Nivritti paths, he shuns the one fraught with pain, and follows the other full of bliss, and thus reaches the highest Turiya stage beyond both of them.

आशाम्बरो न नमस्कारो न स्वधाकारो न निन्दा न स्तुतिर्यादृच्छिको भवेद्भिक्षुर्नाऽऽवाहनं न विसर्जनं न मन्त्रं न ध्यानं नोपासनं च न लक्ष्यं नालक्ष्यं न पृथग्नापृथगहं न न त्वं न सर्वं चानिकेतस्थितिरेव भिक्षुः सौवर्णादीनां नैव परिग्रहेन्न लोकं नावलोकं चाऽऽबाधकः क इति चेद्- बाधकोऽस्त्येव यस्माद्भिक्षुर्हिरण्यं रसेन दृष्टं च स ब्रह्महा भवेत् । यस्माद्भिक्षुर्हिरण्यं रसेन स्पृष्टं च स पौल्कसो भवेत् । यस्माद्भिक्षुर्हिरण्यं रसेन ग्राह्यं च स आत्महा भवेत् । तस्माद्भिक्षुर्हिरण्यं रसेन न दृष्टं च न स्पृष्टं च न ग्राह्यं च ।

सर्वे कामा मनोगता व्यावर्तन्ते ।   दुःखे नोद्विग्नः सुखे न
स्पृहा त्यागो रागे सर्वत्र शुभाशुभयोरनभिस्नेहो न द्वेष्टि
न मोदं च ।   सर्वेषामिन्द्रियाणां गतिरुपरमते य आत्मन्ये-
वावस्थीयते यत्पूर्णानन्दैकबोधस्तद्ब्रह्माहमस्मीति कृतकृत्यो
भवति कृतकृत्यो भवति ॥४॥

4.   The quarters are his clothing, he prostrates himself
before none,[1] he offers[2] no oblation to the Pitris (manes),
blames none, praises none—the Sannyāsin is ever of
independent will.[3]   For ·him there is no invocation to
God,[4] no valedictory ceremony[5] to him ; no Mantra, no
meditation, no worship ; to him is neither the phenomenal
world[6] nor That which is unknowable ; he sees neither[7]
duality nor does he perceive unity.   He sees neither "I"
nor "thou"[8], nor all this.[9]   The Sannyāsin[10] has no home.[11]
He should not accept anything made of gold or the like, he
should not have a body of disciples, or accept wealth.[12]
If it be asked what harm there is in accepting them, (the
reply is) yes,   there   is harm[13] in doing so.   Because if
the   Sannyāsin   looks   at gold with longing, he makes
himself a killer of Brahman ;[14] because if the Sannyāsin
touches gold with longing, he becomes degraded into a
Chandala ;[15] because if he takes gold with longing, he makes
himself a killer of the Ātman.[16]   Therefore, the Sannyāsin
must neither look at, nor touch nor take gold, with longing.[17]
All desires[18] of the mind cease to exist, (and consequently)
he is not agitated by grief, and has no longing for happiness ;
renunciation of attachment to sense-pleasures comes, and he
is everywhere unattached in good or evil, (consequently)
he neither hates nor is elated.[19] The outgoing tendency
of all the sense-organs subsides in him who rests[20] in
the Ātman alone.   Realising "I am that Brahman who
is the One Infinite Knowledge-Bliss" he reaches the end
of his desires, verily he reaches the end of his desires.[21]

1   *None*—No Devas or the like.

2   *Offers etc.*—He is not required to perform the Shrāddha ceremony.

3   *Independent will*—By his successful practice of detachment of the Self from all objects, and his relinquishing both good and evil, the Paramahamsa, is not dominated by the will of gaining anything for himself, but rests ever content with whatever comes to him of itself.

4   *Invocation to God*—in any image.

5   *Valedictory ceremony*—Prayers offered to the Chosen Deity, at the end of worship, to retire to His Supreme Abode.

6   *Phenomenal world*—in its gross and subtle aspects as conceived by the senses and the mind.

7   *Neither sees etc.*—for he has become the Absolute.

8   *"I" nor "thou"*—He sees not the Self as individualised in himself or in others, but in Its true essence.

9   *All this*—the universe as existing in Brahman, as he has no separate idea of This and That.

10   *The Sannyāsin etc.*—Having dwelt thus far on the nature of the illuminated Paramahamsas, the Upanishad speaks now of the duties of those Sannyāsins who are yet striving to reach the goal.

11   *Has no home*—builds no home (Math) for himself, lest he becomes attached to it ; and consequently he does not live in the same place.   In fact, he should not know where he will sleep next.

12   *Wealth*—Such as, oxen, fields, rest-house for travellers, pilgrims, etc.

13   *Harm*—according to the Shāstras.

14   *Killer of Brahman etc.*—i.e. by his denying Brahman as the only Reality and all else as unreal, he makes Brahman a nonentity to him.

15   *Chandāla*—a person of the untouchable castes.

16   *Killer of the Ātman*—By his attachment to gold and thinking himself as its enjoyer, he kills the true nature of the Self in him, which is unattached, infinite, and is ever the non-enjoyer. Says the Smriti: "Who thinks the Ātman as being otherwise than what It really is, what sin is there which is not done by that thief, the killer of the Self ?"

17   *With longing*—Which implies that the Sannyāsin should not likewise hear and talk about gold, or extol it, or make use of it, in any way, for his self-created needs.

18   *All desires etc.*—The great results which follow one after another by the renunciation of gold are now stated.

19 *Neither hates etc.*—neither hates his enemies, nor is elated by any friend's treating him with the utmost consideration, because he has risen above the ideas of "friend and foe", "likes and dislikes".

20 *Rests etc.*—The Smriti thus extols the bliss such a one possesses: "The happiness enjoyed by the king of the gods, or by the sovereign ruler of all men, is nothing compared with that which belongs to the Yogi who is devoid of attachment and is steadfast in the knowledge of the Self."

21 *End of his desires.*—He has nothing more to desire, no want to satisfy, no duty unperformed. The Shruti says: "The Yogi who is satisfied with the nectar of Self-knowledge, who has reached the end of desires, has no more any duty which is yet to be performed. If he feels the reverse, he is not a knower of Truth."

ॐ भद्रं कर्णेभिः श्रृणुयाम देवाः० । स्वस्ति नो० ।
ॐ शान्तिः शान्तिः शान्तिः । हरिः ॐ ॥
इति श्रीपरमहंसोपनिषत्समाप्ता ॥

Here ends the Paramahamsopanishad with the Shāntipātha "Om ! O Devas," etc. (see p. 1.)

ĀTMOPANISHAD

After Brahmā had propounded to the Devarshis, in the preceding discourse of the Atharva-Veda, the truth about rebirth, Angiras shows in this Upanishad, the way to be free from rebirth, from the bondage of Samsāra, once for all, to those who so desired, by inculcating the Highest Ātman, who is ever taintless and beyond all bondage of birth and death. Angiras was one of the Seven Rishis, a Prajāpati or progenitor of mankind, and one of the ten mind-born sons of Brahmā. Besides being regarded as the priest of the gods, and Lord of Sacrifices he was also a teacher of Brahmavaidyā, to whom many hymns of the Rigveda are ascribed.

The method adopted here is what is technically called शाखाचन्द्रन्यायः —the maxim of the bough and the moon. Just as the moon, though immensely distant from the bough of the tree, is pointed out to a child as the moon *on* the bough, because she appears to be contiguous to it, even so the Paramātman—though He has really no relation with the body and the mind, still for the sake of ease to the learner —is first pointed out through the body and the mind, which are called here, the Outer and the Inner Ātman respectively, because of His appearing very much akin to them to a child-mind. Thus by leading the seeker after Truth step by step, the real nature of the Ātman is disclosed.

ॐ अथैवाङ्गिरास्त्रिविधः पुरुषस्तद्यथा बाह्यात्माऽन्त-
रात्मा परमात्मा चेति । त्वक्चर्मनखमांसरोमाङ्गुल्यङ्-
गुष्ठपृष्ठवंशनखगुल्फोदरनाभिमेढ्रकट्यूरुकपोलभ्रूललाटबाहूपार्श्व-

शिरोधमनिकाक्षीणि श्रोत्राणि भवन्ति जायते म्रियत इत्येष
बाह्यात्मा नाम ॥१॥

1. Om. Then Angiras (said) : The Purusha[1] is
threefold,[2] viz—the Outer-Ātman, the Inner-Ātman and
the Paramātman. The two layers of skin (epidermis and
dermis), the nails[3], the flesh, the hair, the fingers and thumbs,
the backbone, the nails, the ankles, the belly, the navel,
the hips, thighs, the cheeks, and the eyebrows, the forehead
and the arms, the sides, the head, the small veins and
nerves, the eyes, and ears, etc.—that which has these,[4] and
which is born and dies,[5] is called the Outer-Ātman.[6]

1 *The Purusha*—The dweller in the body.

2 *Is threefold*—Though the distinction usually, made in the
Shāstras is fourfold viz—the body, the mind, the Jivātman and the
Paramātman, still considering the identity of the two last, the distinction
is spoken of as threefold here.

3 *Nails*—The repetition of the word is for distinguishing the
nails of the hand from those of the toes.

4 *That which etc.*—i.e. the human body.

5 *Is born and dies*—implies that it also undergoes the four intermediate stages of modification as enumerated by Yāska, viz that it
exists, it changes, it develops, and it decays.

6 *The Outer-Ātman.*—Because the Ātman is identified, in its gross
aspect, with the body, as in the case of one who feels, "*I am* hurt",
"*I* enjoy", according as one meets injury or feels pleasing sensations in it.

अथान्तरात्मा नाम पृथिव्यप्तेजोवाय्वाकाशेच्छाद्वेषसुखदुःख-
काममोहविकल्पनादिभिः स्मृतिलिङ्ग उदात्तानुदात्तह्रस्वदीर्घ-
प्लुतस्खलितगर्जितस्फुटितमुदितनृत्यगीतवादित्रप्रलयविजृम्भिता-
दिभिः श्रोता घ्राता रसयिता मन्ता बोद्धा कर्ता
विज्ञानात्मा पुरुषः पुराणं न्यायो मीमांसा धर्मशास्त्राणीति
श्रवणघ्राणाकर्षणकर्मविशेषणं करोत्येषोऽन्तरात्मा नाम ॥२॥

2. Now, about the Inner-Ātman[1] : Verily He is the Purusha who by his perceiving the earth,[2] water, fire, air, and ether, desire[3] and aversion, pleasure and pain, lust,[4] delusion,[5] doubt etc.—who by his perceiving acute[6] and grave (accents), short,[7] long, and protracted (vowels), and faltered,[8] shouted, abruptly broken, and mixed (syllables), and who by his sensibility to dancing, music, vocal and instrumental, loss[9] of consciousness, yawning etc.—is the the hearer, smeller, taster, thinker, comprehender, doer, and discriminating self, whose sign is memory,[10] (who studies) the Purānas, the Nyāya, the Mimāmsās,[11] and the Dharmashastras and who particularises hearing, smelling, and attracting, from generality of actions—He is called the Inner-Ātman.

1 *Inner-Ātman*—This comprehends the whole range of material phenomena, gross, and subtle (i.e. mental), with which the individual soul concerns himself. It may be well to point out here that according to Hindu philosophy, the mind is nothing but subtle matter.

2 *Earth etc.*—Gross matter, coming under cognition.

3 *Desire etc.*—The pairs of opposites, coming under feeling.

4 *Lust*—implies the other passions—anger, avarice, pride, and envy.

5 *Delusion*—which arises out of blind attachment to worldly objects and sense-enjoyments, and prevents one from discerning the truth.

6 *Acute and grave (accents)*—By mentioning the Udātta (high) and the Anudātta (low) in the series of tones, intermediate mixed tone, the Svarita, is also implied.

7 *Short etc.*—These are the three kinds of vowel sounds used in Sanskrit prosody.

8 *Faltered etc.*—These are the defects in pronunciation of syllables, or in speech.

9 *Loss of consciousness*—considered as one of the thirty-three subordinate feelings.

10 *Memory*—It is the chief characteristic of individual self, for without it he should forget in youth what he experienced in boyhood, the body having undergone a thorough change. Here Chitta or the mind-stuff comes into play, storing up all the past impressions in a subtle form and bringing them to the surface when stimulated.

11 *Mimāmsās*—The Purva-Mimāmsā of Jaimini, and the Uttara-Mimāmsā, or the Vedanta, of Vyāsa.

12 *Dharmashāstras*—The codes of laws compiled by the Rishis.

अथ परमात्मा नाम यथाक्षरमुपासनीयः । स च
प्राणायामप्रत्याहारसमाधियोगानुमानाध्यात्मचिन्तकं वट-
कणिका श्यामाकतण्डुलो बालाग्रशतसहस्रविकल्पनादिभि-
र्नं लभ्यते नोपलभ्यते । न जायते म्रियते न शुष्यते न
दह्यति न कम्पते न भिद्यते न च्छिद्यते निर्गुणः साक्षी-
भूतः । शुद्धो निरवयवात्मा केवलः सूक्ष्मो निष्कलो
निरञ्जनो निरभिमानः शब्दस्पर्शरसरूपगन्धर्वजितो
निर्विकल्पो निराकाङक्षः सर्वव्यापी सोऽचिन्त्योऽवर्ण्यश्च
पुनात्यशुद्धान्यपूतानि निष्क्रियः संस्कारो नास्ति संस्कारो
नास्त्येष परमात्मा पुरुषो नाम ॥३॥

3. Now about the Paramātman : Verily He is to
be worshipped[1] according[2] to the precepts of the Vedas.
And He (reveals Himself) to one who, through the Yoga[3]
of Prānāyāma[4], Pratyāhāra,[5] and samādhi,[6] or through
reasoning[7] meditates on the Adhyātma.[8] He is like the
banyan seed,[9] or like the Shyāmāka grain ;[10] conceived
of as being as subtle as a hundred thousandth fraction of
the point of a hair, and so forth. He cannot be grasped or
perceived.[11] He is not born,[12] He does not die ; He is
neither dried up, nor burnt, nor shaken, nor pierced,
nor severed ; He is beyond all qualities,[13] the Witness,
eternal pure,[14] of the essence of the indivisible,[15] one-only
subtle, without components, without taint,[16] without egoism[17]
devoid of sound,[18] touch, taste, sight, and smell, devoid of doubt,[19] without expectation ;[20] He is all-pervading,[21]
unthinkable, indescribable,[22] He purifies the unclean[23]
and the defiled ;[24] He is without action ; He has no Sams-

kāras,[25] He has no Samskāras—He is the Purusha who is called the Paramātman.

1 *Worshipped*—realised in His true essence.

2 *According etc.*—The Paramātman is to be sought only through the Vedas, or the Revealed Knowledge Eternal, by means of a duly perfected mind.

3 *Yoga*—i.e. Rāja-Yoga.

4 *Prānāyāma*—Lit. control of the Prāna or the sum total of the Cosmic Energy. This is gradually effected by the proper control of breath, the most tangible manifestation of Prāna in the body. This is the fourth step in the course of Yoga practice, coming after Yama and Niyama, or control of external and internal organs, and Āsana (posture).

5 *Pratyāhāra*—The drawing in of organs into the Chitta or mind-stuff, by detaching them from their objects. This follows Prānāyāma.

6 *Samādhi*—including in it its two preceding stages of Dhāranā (concentration) and Dhyāna (meditation). When concentration is perfect the Yogi attains Samādhi and realises the Absolute.

7 *Through reasoning*—i.e. through Jnāna-Yoga, or the process of analysing the real and the unreal, till the ultimate entity is reached.

8 *Adhyātma*—The reality underlying the innermost individual Self. According to Shridhara, the relation between the Jivātman and the Paramātman.

9 *Banyan seed*—Just as this tiny seed brings forth the huge tree, so from the most subtle Ātman emanates the whole universe.

10 *Shyāmāka grain*—which, though very small, shoots forth long stems. The analogy with the Ātman is the same as the above.

11 *Grasped or perceived*—Grasped by the external organs and perceived by the internal organs.

12 *Not born etc.*—By all these negations, every possible action in Him or upon Him is denied ; hence He experiences no sorrow.

13 *Beyond all qualities*—by this every limiting adjunct is denied of Him.

14 *Pure*—by nature, hence devoid of inborn impurity.

15 *Indivisible*—hence devoid of all diversity within Himself.

16 *Taint*—acquired impurity.

17 *Egoism*—all defects arising from Ahamkāra.

18 *Sound etc.*—defects arising from the functions of the external organs.

19 *Doubt*—the defect of the Manas.

20 *Expectation*—defects of the Buddhi, such as hoping, etc.

21   *All-pervading*—Being subtler than the subtlest and greater than the greatest, He pervades everything by His own majesty, and cannot be measured by any means.

22   *Unthinkable, indescribable*—All thought is a limitation. How can therefore the Ātman, the one eternal Subject, be made the object of thought ?

23   *Unclean*—by birth, such as the untouchables etc.

24   *Defiled*—by sin.

25   *He has no Samskāras*—Samskāras being the impression on the mind of works done previously, are impossible in the Absolute Ātman. The repetition marks the close of the discourse.

इत्यथर्ववेद   आत्मोपनिषत्समाप्ता ॥

Here ends the Ātmopanishad contained in the Atharva-Veda.

AMRITABINDUPANISHAD

Of the five Bindu Upanishads, viz the Nādabindu, Brahmabindu, Amritabindu, Dhyānabindu, and Tejabindu, the Amritabindu occupies a very important place sufficiently justifying its title—which literally means "A drop of nectar"—by its felicitous combination of a loftiness of sentiment with a directness of expression. Thus, though it is small in bulk it is nevertheless a drop from the fountain of Eternal Life itself, potent to cure the manifold ills of Samsāra, or the endless rotation of birth and death.

The texts of the Brahmabindu and the Amritabindu Upanishads are virtually the same, with slight alterations in the wording here and there. Taking into consideration the subjectivity of our experience of the outside world, the Amritabindu Upanishad inculcates, first, the control of the mind in the shape of desirelessness for sense-objects, as the most effective way to the attainment of liberation and the realisation of the One who is Knowledge and Bliss Absolute. Then it sets forth in an easy and convincing way the real nature of the soul and the realisation of the highest truth which leads to unity. Thus the central theme of all the Upanishads—viz that the Jiva and Brahman are eternally one, and that all duality is a mere superimposition due to ignorance—finds a clear and forceful emphasis in these terse, epigrammatic verses.

ॐ भद्रं कर्णेभि०। ॐ स्वस्ति न इ०।
ॐ शान्तिः शान्तिः शान्तिः।

(The same Shāntipātha as on page 1).

मनो हि द्विविधं प्रोक्तं शुद्धं चाशुद्धमेव च।
अशुद्धं कामसंकल्पं शुद्धं कामविवर्जितम् ॥१॥

1. The mind is chiefly spoken of as of two kinds,[1]
pure[2] and impure. The impure mind is that which is
possessed of desire,[3] and the pure is that which is devoid
of desire.

1 *Two kinds*—Though the mind has various other states, such
as mixed, insane, etc., two are especially pointed out here.

2 *Pure*—Purified by countless good deeds in past incarnations as
well as by practices of self-control in this.

3 *Possessed of desire*—i.e. entirely dominated by the resolve of
gaining the full measure of enjoyment from all sense-objects.

मन एव मनुष्याणां कारणं बन्धमोक्षयोः ।
बन्धाय विषयासक्तं मुक्तं निर्विषयं स्मृतम् ॥२॥

2. It is indeed the mind that is the cause of men's
bondage and liberation.[1] The mind that is attached to
sense-objects leads to bondage, while dissociated from
sense-objects it tends to lead to liberation. So they[2] think.

1 *Liberation*—The manifestation of the Self as Existence-Knowledge-Bliss Absolute, after the removal of ignorance.

2 *They*—the wise.

यतो निर्विषयस्यास्य मनसो मुक्तिरिष्यते ।
अतो निर्विषयं नित्यं मनः कार्यं मुमुक्षुणा ॥३॥

3. Since liberation is predicated of the mind devoid of
desire[1] for sense-objects, therefore, the mind should always
be made free of such desire, by the seeker after liberation.

1 *Devoid of desire etc.*—Hence, a mere witness of things seen and
perceived.

निरस्तविषयासङ्गं संनिरुद्धं मनो हृदि ।
यदाऽऽप्यात्यात्मनो भावं तदा तत्परमं पदम् ॥४॥

4. When the mind, with its attachment for sense-
objects annihilated, is fully controlled within the heart[1]

and thus realises its own essence², then that Supreme
State (is gained).

The result of such control of mind is given in this Shloka.

1 *Heart*—the seat of pure consciousness.

2 *Its own essence*—The consciousness of the oneness of the individual
soul with the Universal Soul, as "I am He".

तावदेव निरोद्धव्यं यावद्धृदि गतं क्षयम् ।
एतज्ज्ञानं च ध्यानं च शेषो न्यायश्च विस्तरः ॥५॥

5. The mind should be controlled to that extent
in which it gets merged¹ in the heart. This is Jnāna
(realisation) and² this is Dhyāna (meditation) also, all
else is argumentation and verbiage.³

The control of the mind and its concentration is the first step
towards gaining any knowledge, be it about the Ātman or of
the outside world. It is the only key to the treasure-house of all knowledge.

1 *Merged etc.*—i.e. by the realisation of "I am Brahman",
the consciousness of Subject and Object is destroyed.

2 *And*—The two *cha*'s in the text imply other means of
realisation.

3 *Argumentation and verbiage*—by which no real purpose is
served in the path of Mukti. Even scriptures are useless when
concentration of the mind is gained.

नैव चिन्त्यं न चाचिन्त्यं न चिन्त्यं चिन्त्यमेव तत् ।
पक्षपातविनिर्मुक्तं ब्रह्म संपद्यते तदा ॥६॥

6. (The Supreme State) is neither to be thought
of (as being something external and pleasing to the mind),
nor unworthy to be thought of (as something unpleasant
to the mind) ; nor is It to be thought of (as being of the
form of sense-pleasure), but to be thought of (as the essence
of the ever-manifest, eternal, supreme Bliss Itself) ; that
Brahman¹ which is free from all partiality² is attained in
that state.³

3

1 *Brahman*—unconditioned by time, space, and causation.

2 *Free from all partiality*—being equally present in all objects.

3 *In that state*—when the mind is perfectly controlled, and thus free from such activities as draw it out to the world of senses.

This Shloka may also be explained in the following way :

Neither that which is unthinkable—being beyond all phenomenal existence—is to be thought of ; nor is that which is thinkable, i.e. the objective world, to be excluded from thought—to be shunned as being unreal. When the mind becomes free from partiality to either, then Brahman is attained.

The mind becomes free when it ceases to think that this is reality and therefore to be thought of, and this is unreality and therefore to be shunned, and thus recognises no duality.

स्वरेण संधयेद्योगमस्वरं भावयेत्परम् ।
अस्वरेणानुभावेन भावो वाऽभाव इष्यते ।।७।।

7.   One should duly[1] practise concentration on Om (first) through the means of its letters[2], then meditate on Om[3] without regard to its letters.   Finally on the realisation[4] with this latter form of meditation on Om, the idea of the of the non-entity[5] is attained as entity.[6]

The means to be adopted to attain such restraint is given in this Shloka.

1 *Duly*—according to the instruction of the Guru.

2 *Letters*—A, U, M, of which Om is composed ; that is to say, meditate first on what each of these sound-symbols stands for.

3 *On Om etc.*—On the true meaning, or the idea, only that this sacred word-symbol represents, i.e. the Supreme Essence beyond the pale of words.

In the Māndukya Upanishad it is said that Om is all that which has been, all that which is, and is to be, that all is Om, only Om.

4 *Realisation*—"I am Brahman".

5 *Non-entity*—of the Avidyā or nescience with its effects, viz the world of name and form.

6 *Entity*—in the absence of Avidyā and all its effects is seen the essence of Brahman free from all limitations and aspects, i.e. Brahman alone remains.

तदेव निष्कलं ब्रह्म निर्विकल्पं निरञ्जनम् ।
तद्ब्रह्माहमिति ज्ञात्वा ब्रह्म संपद्यते ध्रुवम् ॥८॥

8. That alone[1] is Brahman, without component parts,
without doubt[2], and without taint.[3] Realising "I am
that Brahman " one becomes the immutable Brahman.

This Shloka describes Brahman in the "Neti Neti" or negative
method.

1 *That alone*—which reveals Itself on the realisation of the
nonentity of nescience.

2 *Without doubt*—That which does not cogitate as to whether
it is this or that ; or it may mean, "That which is beyond the
conception of things unreal."

3 *Taint*—of Avidyā.

निर्विकल्पमनन्तं च हेतुदृष्टान्तवर्जितम् ।
अप्रमेयमनादि च यज्ज्ञात्वा मुच्यते बुधः ॥९॥

9. (Brahman is) without doubt, endless,[1] beyond
reason and analogy,[2] beyond all proofs[3] and causeless[4]
knowing which the wise one becomes free.

1 *Endless*—not limited by time, causation, and finite matter.

2 *Reason and analogy*—Two of the processes of logical inference.
Brahman cannot be proved by inference.

3 *Beyond all proofs*—Undemonstrable by any mode of proof.

4 *Causeless*—Hence, unaffected by any effect or modification.

न निरोधो न चोत्पत्तिर्न बद्धो न च साधकः ।
न मुमुक्षुर्न वै मुक्त इत्येषा परमार्थता ॥१०॥

10. The highest Truth is that (pure consciousness)
which realises, "There is neither[1] control of the mind, nor
its coming into play", "Neither am I bound, nor am I a
worshipper,[2] neither am I a seeker after liberation, nor one
who has attained liberation".[3]

1 *There is neither etc.*—All these forms of mental consciousness which are negatived here, are unreal from the standpoint of the highest spiritual knowledge. This notion is the intuitive conviction of Consciousness and is the real Truth.

2 *Worshipper*—One who devotes himself to religious practices by adhering to the vows of Brahmacharya and the like.

3 *Liberation*—The ideas such as worshipper, liberation, etc. presuppose bondage which has no place in the eternally free Ātman.

एक एवाऽऽत्मा मन्तव्यो जाग्रत्स्वप्नसुषुप्तिषु ।
स्थानत्रयव्यतीतस्य पुनर्जन्म न विद्यते ॥११॥

11. Verily the Ātman[1] should be known as being the same[2] in Its states of wakefulness,[3] dreaming,[4] and dreamless sleep.[5] For him who has transcended[6] the three states there is no more rebirth.[7]

1 *Ātman*—the self-luminous witness of Buddhi—the Ego-consciousness in everyone.

2 *The same*—Immutable and devoid of distinction.

3 *Wakefulness*—When impressions of the objective world are directly received by the senses.

4 *Dreaming*—When objects are perceived on the subconscious plane through the desire-nature only, i.e. by impressions of past sense-perceptions on the mind.

5 *Dreamless sleep*—When there is a complete cessation of differentiation in impressions and knowledge, and what remains is consciousness alone.

A doubt may be raised that states are due to birth and hence that which has states must also be subject to birth. The second half of the Shloka negates such an idea.

6 *Transcended*—That is, attained the Turiya or superconscious state in which Brahman is realised. The three states enumerated above are unreal, being superimposed upon the Ātman through ignorance of its true nature.

7 *No more rebirth*—than that which It once seemed to have owing to nescience.

एक एव हि भूतात्मा भूते भूते व्यवस्थितः ।
एकधा बहुधा चैव दृश्यते जलचन्द्रवत् ॥१२॥

12.   Being the one,[1] the universal Soul is present in all
beings.[2] Though one, It is seen as many, like the moon[3]
in the water.

1   *One*—without any differentiation whatsoever.

2   *Beings*—human or divine, animate or inanimate.

3   *Moon etc.*—Just as the one moon appears as many by reflection
in different water-vessels.

घटसंवृतमाकाशं नीयमाने घटे यथा ।
घटो नीयेतं नाऽऽकाशं तथा जीवो नभोपमः ॥१३॥

13.   Just as it is the jar which being removed (from one
place to another) changes places and not the Ākāsha[1]
enclosed in the jar—so is the Jiva[2] which resembles[3] the
Ākāsha.

1   *Akāsha*—The all-pervading space.

2   *So is the Jiva*—So does the Self-in-the-individual experience
no change at all, though the Linga-Sharira or the subtle body of
man may be taken after death to various regions, good or bad
according to past Karma.

3   *Resembles*—in its aspect of immutability, and in that of all-
pervasiveness only. Just as the all-pervading Ākāsha does not perish
when the jars which held it are broken, so it is with the all-pervading
Self at the repeated destruction of the body, its Upādhi. The resem-
blance is only thus far, but not as regards consciousness where there is a
difference between the two, as the next shloka shows.

घटवद्विविधाकारं भिद्यमानं पुनः पुनः ।
तद्भग्नं न च जानाति स जानाति च नित्यशः ॥१४॥

14.   When various forms like the jar are broken again
and again the Ākāsha does not know them to be broken,
but He[1] knows perfectly.[2]

1   *He*—the ever-manifest, all-knowing, blissful Self.

2   *Knows perfectly*—that He is ever unborn and deathless.

शब्दमायावृतो नैव तमसा याति पुष्करे ।
भिन्ने तमसि चैकत्वमेक एवानुपश्यति ॥१५॥

15.   Being covered by Māya,[1] which is a mere sound,
It does not, through darkness, know the Ākasha (the Blissful
one).   When ignorance is rent asunder, It being then Itself
only[2] sees the unity.[3]

This Shloka explains why it is that the Ātman which is
omniscient is not always aware of Its true nature which is Bliss.

1   *Māyā etc.*—(a) Māyā which is a mere word having no real
(unending) existence ; or (b), Māyā which is the cause of the phenomenal world composed of sound etc.

2   *Itself only*—there being utter absence of the differentiation between the subject and the object.

3   *Unity*—of the individual soul with the Universal Soul.

The purport of the Shloka is this : (a) Just as a man, though
possessed of his senses and faculties, cannot find a particular thing,
however near it may be, if he is blinded by darkness, so the Ātman
does not know Its own nature as Existence-Knowledge-Bliss through the
covering of Māyā.   Or (b), just as the Ākāsha shut up within the jar
knows not that it is the same as the infinite Ākāsha, so the individual
soul being covered by the darkness of Māyā does not know its real nature.   When the jar is broken, there remains the one infinite Ākāsha ;
similarly, when the covering of Māyā is rent asunder by Jnāna,
the Ātman shines in Its own essence of One-only-without-a-second.

शब्दाक्षरं परं ब्रह्म तस्मिन्क्षीणे यदक्षरम् ।
तद्विद्वानक्षरं ध्यायेद्यदीच्छेच्छान्तिमात्मनः ॥१६॥

16.   The Om as Word is (first looked upon as) the
Supreme Brahman.   After that (word-idea) has vanished,
that imperishable Brahman (remains).   The wise one
should meditate[1] on that imperishable Brahman, if he
desires the peace[2] of his soul.

The Upanishad continues the topic of the means to the realisation it
had commenced in Shloka 7.

1   *Meditate etc.*—as "I am Brahman".

2   *Peace*—in the form of the annihilation of all misery caused by
Avidyā, i.e. the state of Moksha.

द्वे विद्ये वेदितव्ये तु शब्दब्रह्म परं च यत् ।
शब्दब्रह्मणि निष्णातः परं ब्रह्माधिगच्छति ॥१७॥

17. Two kinds of Vidyā[1] ought to be known—the Word-Brahman[2] and the Supreme Brahman. One having mastered[3] the Word-Brahman attains to the Highest Brahman.

1 *Two kinds of Vidyā*—the Aparā or lower, and the Parā or the higher. Realisation of the Self is Parā-vidyā, and all other forms of knowledge are Aparā-vidyā. The latter are also Vidyā because they dispel Avidyā or ignorance in a way, but they are subsidiary to the former.

2 *Word-Brahman*—The Vedas with the Upavedas etc. With each of the four Vedas is attached an Upaveda ; thus we have the sciences of medicine, warfare, music, and mechanics.

3 *Mastered etc.*—Nishnāta : Lit. plunged deeply into. Assimilated the spirit of the Vedas by proper study, discipline, and contemplation. It helps the realisation of the Highest Brahman and hence its importance.

ग्रन्थमभ्यस्य मेधावी ज्ञानविज्ञानतत्परः ।
पलालमिव धान्यार्थी त्यजेद्ग्रन्थमशेषतः ॥१८॥

18. After studying the Vedas the intelligent one who is solely intent on acquiring knowledge and realisation,[1] should discard[2] the Vedas altogether, as the man who seeks to obtain rice discards the husk.

1 *Knowledge and realisation*—Knowledge, by a study of the scriptures, and realisation, the perception of Brahman (Brahma-sākshātkāra), by a practical application of the highest truths thereof, through the instructions of the Guru.

2 *Discard etc.*—When he knows that a mere study of the Vedas and the performance of the Karma-kānda inculcated therein cannot bring on the utter annihilation of Samsāra, and that the end of the Vedas is the realisation of the Self, he gives up the former as no more needful and exclusively devotes himself to the latter.

गवामनेकवर्णानां क्षीरस्याप्येकवर्णता ।
क्षीरवत्पश्यते ज्ञानं लिङ्गिनस्तु गवां यथा ॥१९॥

19. Of cows which are of diverse colours the milk is of the same colour. (The intelligent one) regards Jnāna as the milk, and the many-branched Vedas as the cows.

The Vedas have numerous recensions, but each of these sets forth the same highest Truth, "Thou art That" in different words. The "milk" (Jñāna) is the chief concern of the cowherd (seeker after Truth), the "colour of the cows", of the book-learned.

घृतमिव पयसि निगूढं भूते भूते वसति विज्ञानम् ।
सततं मन्थयितव्यं मनसा मन्थानभूतेन ॥२०॥

20. Like the butter hidden[1] in milk, the Pure Consciousness[2] resides in every being. That ought to be constantly churned out[3] by the churning rod of the mind.

If the mind is not controlled, the knowledge "Thou art That" does not manifest itself in it.

1 *Hidden*—pervades every particle of the milk in the jar, in the unmanifested form, before being churned.

2 *Pure Consciousness*—The Ātman, the essence of knowledge and bliss.

3 *Churned out*—should be made manifest by means of constant meditation and discrimination ("Neti, Neti" process).

ज्ञाननेत्रं समादाय उद्धरेद्वह्निवत्परम् ।
निष्कलं निश्चलं शान्तं तद्ब्रह्माहमिति स्मृतम् ॥२१॥

21. Taking hold of the rope of knowledge, one should bring out, like fire,[1] the Supreme Brahman. I am that Brahman indivisible, immutable, and calm, thus it is thought of.[2]

1 *Like fire*—Just as fire is produced by churning at a sacrifice.

Here, the mind is the rod, the knowledge which sees the unity of the Jiva and Brahman is the rope, and the constant meditation is the churning, the friction, which brings out the "fire", i.e. leads to the realisation of the Paramātman.

2 *Thought of*—by men of realisation.

सर्वभूताधिवासं यद्भूतेषु च वसत्यपि ।
सर्वानुग्राहकत्वेन तदस्म्यहं वासुदेवस्तदस्म्यहं
वासुदेव इति ॥२२॥

22. In Whom reside all beings, and Who resides in all beings by virtue of His being the giver of grace to all—I am that Soul of the universe, the Supreme Being, I am that[1] Soul of the Universe, the Supreme Being.

1 *I am that etc.*—Hence dawns the realisation that all beings reside in me and I in them. The repetition indicates the close of the Upanishad.

ॐ भद्रं कर्णेभिः॰ ।   ॐ स्वस्ति न इ॰ ।

ॐ शान्तिः शान्तिः शान्तिः ।

इत्यथर्ववेदेऽमृतबिन्दूपनिषत्समाप्ता ॥

(The same Shantipath as on page 1).

Here ends the Amritabindupanishad as contained in the Atharva-Veda.

TEJABINDUPANISHAD

The Tejabindupanishad is the last of the five Bindu
Upanishads forming part of the Atharva-Veda. It con-
ceives the Supreme Ātman dwelling in the heart of man, as
the most subtle centre of effulgence, revealed only to Yogis
by supersensuous meditation. After stating the disciplines
which the Truth-seeker must undergo in order to master
that most difficult but the only process of supreme realisation, the Tejabindu sets forth, in the highest philosophical
conceptions, the nature of That which is to be meditated
upon, and realised in essence, that is to say, Brahman,
the Absolute, and points out in conclusion some of the
disqualifications which the student must shun if he desires
to be "one of those who make the inaccessible accessible"
and reach the goal, the absolute freedom of the soul.

ॐ तेजबिन्दुः परं ध्यानं विश्वातीतं हृदि स्थितम् ।
आणवं शांभवं शाक्तं स्थूलं सूक्ष्मं परं च यत् ॥१॥

1. Om. (Now about) the Effulgent Point :[1] It has
its excellent meditation : Supermundane,[2] seated in the
heart, (attainable by) the Ānava,[3] Shākta and Shāmbhava
(methods) ; (the meditation is) gross,[4] subtle, as well as
that which is transcendental.

1 *The Effulgent Point*—The indwelling Ātman is meant. *Effulgent*—
Because of Its being the Light of lights, physical and spiritual, It
illumines the whole universe and dispels all darkness of the mind.
Point—denoting Its extreme subtleness ; hence It cannot be grasped by
the mind which is not purified and concentrated.

2 *Supermundane*—Beyond the phenomenal.

3 *Ānava etc.*—These are the three ways of initiation mentioned
in the scriptures. The first, the Ānava, is the ordinary mode in
which the Guru communicates to his disciple a Mantra (a sacred

formula, which the latter, is called upon to regularly repeat and
meditate upon) and instructs him in the ways of worship, posture,
and meditation. The second, the Shākta, is much higher and is
imparted by perfected souls who by their own power can instil
the higher spiritual consciousness in the disciple without his having
had to go through any external modes of worship to attain to it.
But the third, the Shāmbhava, is the highest mode in which the
greatest Teachers of humanity whose mercy knows no reason, raise
the disciple at once to the highest stage of realisation.

4 *Gross etc.*—These three meditations correspond respectively
to the above three modes of initiation. Transcendental, i.e. so subtle
in its working that it cannot be accounted for by human reasoning.

दुःसाध्यं च दुराराध्यं दुष्प्रेक्ष्यं च दुराश्रयम् ।
दुर्लक्षं दुस्तरं ध्यानं मुनीनां च मनीषिणाम् ॥२॥

2.   Even to the wise and the thoughtful this meditation
is difficult to perform, and difficult to attain, difficult to
congnise and difficult to abide in, difficult to define and
difficult to cross.[1]

1   *Difficult to cross*—Whose end is difficult to be reached.

जिताहारो जितक्रोधो जितसङ्गो जितेन्द्रियः ।
निर्द्वन्द्वो निरहंकारो निराशीरपरिग्रहः ॥३॥

3.   (To attain that meditation one has to be) abstemious
in food,[1] a master over anger, attachment and his passions;
(one has to be) free from the pairs of opposites,[2] devoid of
egoism, free from hope, and free from possession.[3]

1   *Abstemious in food*—i.e. to be moderate in food and take only
such as is good for his body and conducive to mental purity.

2   *Pairs of opposites*—viz heat and cold, good and bad, pleasure
and pain, success and failure. All that can be classed under
upādeya—rejectable or acceptable.

3   *Free from possession*—Aparigraha : or it may mean, one who
does not receive gifts. This non-receiving is one of the several kinds
of Yamas, or mental restraints, mentioned in the Yoga Shāstra by
Patanjali, for the acquirement of independence and purity of thought.

अगम्यगम्यकर्ता च गुरुमानार्थमानसः ।
मुखानि त्रीणि विन्दन्ति त्रिधामा हंस उच्यते ॥४॥

4. (He should be) one[1] who makes that which is inaccessible accessible, one whose whole aim is to serve[2] the Guru and his cause only. (Sages) reach the three gates[3] (to It). (Therefore) the Supreme Soul is said to have three resorts.[4]

1 *One etc.*—i.e. he must be a person of indomitable energy and perseverance, who undaunted by difficulties on the path, however great will reach the goal.

2 *Serve the Guru etc.*—Gurumānārthamānasah of the text may also be explained as : one whose whole end and aim is the worship of the Supreme Spirit.

3 *Three gates*—three means of attainment, viz Vairāgya, dispassion (as implied in verse 3), and Utsāha, zeal and Gurubhakti, devotion to the Guru (as stated in the preceding part of this Shloka).

4 *Three resorts*—Tridhāmā : Three accesses. Or, three states of waking, dreaming and dreamless sleep in which the soul resides.

परं गुह्यमिदं स्थानमव्यक्तं ब्रह्म निराश्रयम् ।
व्योमरूपं कलासूक्ष्मं विष्णोस्तत्परमं पदम् ॥५॥

5. This is supreme, hidden in mystery, the resting-place (of all) and imperceptible ; it is Brahman, without support,[1] of the nature of unlimited space, atomic,[2] and subtle. That is the supreme abode[3] of Vishnu.[4]

This and the succeeding six Shlokas set forth the nature of That which is to be meditated upon, viz Brahman or Ātman.

1 *Without support*—Brahman being bigger than the biggest, cannot have anything to support it.

2 *Atomic*—indivisible and incomprehensively minute.

3 *Abode*—Pada :   State.

4 *Vishnu*—Derived from its root-meaning Vish, it means That which pervades or indwells all.

त्र्यम्बकं त्रिगुणं स्थानं त्रिधातु रूपवर्जितम् ।
निश्चलं निर्विकल्पं च निराधारं निराश्रयम् ॥६॥

6. Pertaining to the Tryambaka,[1] containing, the three Gunas,[2] support (of all) ; the three worlds[3] are its elementary or essential constituents ; devoid of form, unchangeable, unconditioned, uncontainable, and without substratum.

1 *Tryambaka*—Lit. having three eyes. The Father of the three worlds, or the Revealer of the three Vedas.

2 *The three Gunas*—viz Sattva, Rajas, and Tamas.

3 The three worlds—viz Bhuh, Bhuvah, and Svah—the universe, the etherial space, and the heaven.

उपाधिरहितं स्थानं वाङ्मनोऽतीतगोचरम् ।
स्वभावभावनाग्राह्यं संघातैकपदोज्झितम् ॥७॥

7. It is the State free from all limitations, beyond the range of speech and mind perceivable by thinking on one's own state,[1] and abandoned[2] by words denoting plurality as well as unity.

1 *State*—real nature free from all false identifications with the self.

2 *Abandoned* etc.—because of their inability to express Its real nature.

The original text may also be explained as : Inaccessible to one who has made the body and the senses his all-in-all.

आनन्दं नन्दनातीतं दुष्प्रेक्ष्यमजमव्ययम् ।
चित्तवृत्तिविनिर्मुक्तं शाश्वतं ध्रुवमच्युतम् ॥८॥

8. (It is) Bliss itself, beyond[1] the causality of happiness, difficult to be seen, birthless, immutable, free from all functions of the mind-stuff, eternal, constant and imperishable.

1 *Beyond* etc.—Being Bliss itself, nothing external can impart bliss to Brahman.

तद्ब्रह्माणं तदध्यात्मं तन्निष्ठा तत्परायणम् ।
अचित्तचित्तमात्मानं तद्व्योम परमं स्थितम् ॥९॥

9. It is That which is Brahman, It is That which
is Adhyātma,[1] It is That which is the extreme limit,[2]
It is That which is the supreme refuge ; It is knowledge[3]
independent of the mind-stuff, It is the Ātman, It is of
the nature of infinite space ; established (in all actions).[4]

1 *Adhyātma*—The Reality which makes up the inner-most individual
self.

2 *Extreme limit*—the perfection to which anything can reach.

3 *Knowledge etc.*—Lit. it is that Chitta which is not-Chitta, i.e.
which is not identified with its modifications but remains in its own pure
essence of knowledge self-manifest.

4 *Established (in all actions)*—as their efficient guide.

अशून्ये शून्यभावं च शून्यातीतमवस्थितम् ।
न ध्यानं न च वा ध्याता न ध्येयो ध्येय एव च ॥१०॥

10. Though It is that which is not void,[1] yet thought[2]
of as void,[3] (but in reality) It transcends voidness, and is
firm-fixed.[4] There is[5] neither thinker, nor thought nor the
thinkable. Still it is to be meditated upon.[6]

1 *Not void*—being the Whole by Itself.

2 *Thought of*—erroneously, by the ignorant and the materialistic.

3 *As void*—as absolutely non-existent.

4 *Firm-fixed*—being the Whole.

5 *There is etc.*—because of Its being the Absolute, above cause
and effect.

6 *Meditated upon*—as conferring upon men final liberation.

सर्वं तत्परमं शून्यं न परं परमात्परम् ।
अचिन्त्यमप्रबुद्धं च न च सत्यं न संविदुः ॥
मुनीनां तत्त्वयुक्तं तु न देवा न परं विदुः ॥११॥

11. That (Brahman) is All, Supreme, of the
nature of space, to It there is nothing superior ; it is

higher than the highest, unthinkable, and free from the experiences of the waking state. It is not that the sages who devote themselves to the Truth[2] do not know It as the Reality. It is not also that the gods do not know the Highest.

1 *Nature etc.*—being unattached.

2 *Truth*—as stated in the preceding Shlokas.

लोभं मोहं भयं दर्पं कामं क्रोधं च किल्बिषम् ।
शीतोष्णं क्षुत्पिपासं च संकल्पं च विकल्पकम् ।
न ब्रह्मकुलदर्पं च न मुक्तिं ग्रन्थसंचयम् ॥१२॥

12. (Brahman is) not (known to those who are possessed of) avarice, delusion, fear, egotism, lust, anger, and sin[1] or (possessed of) heat and cold,[2] hunger and thirst, or mental resolve and indecision, or pride of birth[3] in a Brāhmana family, or (vanity in having read) a mass of books on Mukti.

1 *Sin*—Kilbisham : It may also mean, disease.

2 (*Possessed of*) *heat and cold*—unable to bear heat, cold, etc. with equanimity.

3 *Birth etc.*—Realisation is not dependent on birth or book-learning as has been repeatedly demonstrated in the lives of saints, from the very earliest times to our own day.

न भयं सुखदुःखं च तथा मानापमानयोः ।
एतद्द्वाविविनिर्मुक्तं तद्ग्राह्यं ब्रह्म तत्परं
तद्ग्राह्यं ब्रह्म तत्परमिति ॥१३॥

13. (Brahman is) not (known to those who are sensitive to) fear,[1] or pleasure and pain, or honour and disgrace. (To one) free from these ideas, that Supreme Brahman becomes manifest—to one whose highest refuge[2] is Brahman ; yea, that Supreme Brahman becomes manifest to one whose highest refuge is Brahman.

1 (*Sensitive to*) *fear*—Who are afraid of adverse criticism from others about their conduct.   The proper spirit consists in doing what one thinks to be right, irrespective of the opinion of others.

2 *Highest refuge etc.*—Who is absorbed in, or intent on the contemplation of Brahman.

इत्यथर्ववेदे   तेजबिन्दूपनिषत्समाप्ता ॥

Here ends the Tejabindupanishad, as contained in the Atharva-Veda.

SARVOPANISHAD

The Sarvopanishad is appropriately spoken of as the quintessence of the Upanishads, being a concise and at the same time highly eloquent presentation of the concentrated wisdom, bearing on the main points at issue, of the Vedanta philosophy. The Upanishad opens with questions as to the nature of the twenty-three fundamental topics, and furnishes the answers to them, in a consecutive order, to the end. Starting with bondage and Moksha and their causes, the seeker after truth is treated to a fine and delicate discrimination of the various gross and subtle states, in and through which the soul seems to appear within us, because of its Upādhis. Indicating the real nature of the soul and dealing with the niceties of the ideas conveyed by each of the words of the Mahāvākya Tat-Tvam-Asi (That thou art), the Upanishad seeks to point out the identity of the Jivātman with the Paramāt-man or Supreme Brahman which is spoken of as the Essence of Truth, Knowledge, Infinitude, and Bliss, and concludes by an attempt at defining Māyā, thus completing as it were the circle in order to show what causes the bondage and how it can be broken once for all. From the point of happy definitions of the most difficult and important terms in the phraseology of Vedanta philosophy within the smallest compass, this Upanishad holds a distinct position of its own, and is worthy of our best attention.

ॐ कथं बन्धः कथं मोक्षः काऽविद्या का विद्येति जाग्रत्स्वप्नं सुषुप्तं तुरीयं च कथमन्नमयः प्राणभयो मनोमयो विज्ञानमय आनन्दमयः कथं कर्त्ता जीवः क्षेत्रज्ञः साक्षी कूटस्थोऽन्तर्यामी कथं प्रत्यगात्मा परमात्माऽऽत्मा माया चेति कथमात्मेश्वरोऽनात्मनो देहादीनात्मत्वेनाभिमन्यते

4

सोऽभिमान आत्मनो बन्धस्तन्निवृत्तिर्मोक्षस्तदभिमानं
कारयति या साऽविद्या सोऽभिमानो ययाऽभिनिवर्तते
सा विद्या । मनआदिचतुर्दशकरणैः पुष्कलैरादित्याद्यनु-
गृहीतैः शब्दादीन्विषयान्स्थूलान्यदोपलभते तदाऽऽत्मनो
जागरणं तद्वासनारहितश्चतुर्भिः करणैः शब्दाद्यभावेऽपि
वासनामयाञ्शब्दादीन्यदोपलभते तदाऽऽत्मनः स्वप्नम् ।
चतुर्दशकरणोपरमादिविशेषविज्ञानाभावाद्यदा तदाऽऽत्मनः
सुषुप्तम् ॥१॥

1. Om. What is Bandha (bondage of the Soul)?
What is Moksha (liberation)? What is Avidyā (nescience)?
What is Vidyā (knowledge)? What are the states of Jāgrat
(waking), Svapna (dreaming), Sushupti (Dreamless sleep),
and the fourth, Turiya (Absolute)? What are the Annamaya, Prānamaya, Manomaya, Vijnānamaya, and Ānan-
damaya Koshas (vestures or sheaths of the soul)? What is
the Kartā (agent), what the Jiva (individual self), the
Kshetrajna (knower of the body), the Sākshi (Witness),
the Kutastha, the Antaryāmin (Internal Ruler)? What
is the Pratyagātman (Inner Self), what the Paramātman
(Supreme Self), the Ātman, and also Māyā ?—The master
of Self[1] looks upon the body and such like things other than
the Self as Itself : this egoism[2] is the bondage of the soul.
The cessation of that (egoism) is Moksha, liberation.
That which causes that egoism is Avidyā, nescience. That
by which this egoism is completely turned back[3] is Vidyā,
knowledge.[4] When the self, by means of its four and ten
organs[5] of sense beginning with the mind and be-
nignly influenced[6] by the sun and the rest[7] which appear
outside, perceives gross objects such as sound[8] etc., then
it is the Ātman's Jāgrat (wakeful) state. When, even
in the absence of sound etc.,[9] (the self) not divested[10] of
desire for them, experiences, by means of the four organs,[11]
sound and the rest in the form of desires—then it is the

Ātman's state of Svapna (dream). When the four and ten organs cease from activity, and there is the absence of differentiated knowledge,[12] then is the Ātman's state of Sushupti (dreamless sleep).

1   *The master of Self*—The Paramātman dwelling in the body, as its lord or controller.

2   *This egoism*—This misconception which makes one think, "I am a Brāhmana", "I am beautiful in appearance", "I am the doer of actions", and so on.

3   *Turned back*—towards the Self as the real Ego.

4   *Knowledge*—Spiritual illumination.

5   *Four and ten organs*—The four "inner" organs, viz mind (Manas), intellect (Buddhi), memory (Chitta), and egoism (Ahamkāra) ; the five organs of perception, viz hearing, touch, sight, taste, and smell ; and the five organs of action, such as the tongue, the hand, the leg, etc.

6   *Influenced*—in the matter of resolve, perseverance, perception, and egoism.

7   *Sun etc.*—the Moon, Vishnu, Shiva, the Creator, the Quarters, Air, the Sun, Varuna, the Ashvins, Fire, Indra, Upendra, Mitra, and and Brahmā, who are held to be, respectively, the Adhidevas, or presiding deities, of the fourteen organs of sense enumerated above.

8   *Sound etc.*—i.e. objects that can be heard, touched, seen, tasted, smelt, accepted, rejected, and enjoyed.

9   *Absence of sound etc.*—i.e. though the other organs of sense are inactive.

10   *Not divested etc.*—Tadvāsanārahitah अरहित इति वा छेद: । The thinking in dream comes from desire or attachment to sense-objects, caused by impressions unconsciously left on the mind by the accumulated Karma, good or bad, in past lives, or from current experiences of the waking state. There is said to be another class of dreams which are caused by the instrumentality of the Devas.

11   *Four organs*—the four "inner" organs, viz mind, etc.

12   *Differentiated knowledge*—That is to say, when even the mind and the other inner organs do not function, consciousness by itself alone remains without any object for support.

अवस्थात्रयभावाद्रावसाक्षि   स्वयं   भावाभावरहितं
नैरन्तयं   चैक्यं   यदा   तदा   तत्तुरीयं   चैतन्यमित्युच्यतेऽन-
कार्याणां   षण्णां   कोशानां   समूहोऽन्नमयः   कोश   इत्युच्यते ।

प्राणादिचतुर्दंशवायुभेदा अन्नमये कोशे यदा वर्तन्ते तदा
प्राणमयः कोश इत्युच्यत एतत्कोशद्वयसंयुक्तो मनआदि-
चतुर्भिः करणैरात्मा शब्दादिविषयान्संकल्पादिधर्मान्यदा
करोति तदा मनोमयः कोश इत्युच्यते । एतत्कोशत्रय-
संयुक्तस्तद्गतविशेषाविशेषज्ञो यदाऽवभासते तदा विज्ञान-
मयः कोश इत्युच्यते । एतत्कोशचतुष्टयं स्वकारणज्ञाने
वटकणिकायामिव गुप्तवटवृक्षो यदा वर्तते तदाऽऽनन्द-
मयकोश इत्युच्यते । सुखदुःखबुद्ध्याद्यधयो देहान्तः कर्ता
यदा तदेष्टविषये बुद्धिः सुखबुद्धिरनिष्टविषये बुद्धिर्दुःख-
बुद्धिः शब्दस्पर्शरूपरसगन्धाः सुखदुःखहेतवः । पुण्यपाप-
कर्मानुसारी भूत्वा प्राप्तशरीरसंधिर्योगमप्राप्तशरीरसंयोग-
मिव कुर्वाणो यदा दृश्यते तदोपहितत्वाज्जीव इत्युच्यते ।
मनआदिश्च प्राणादिश्च सत्त्वादिश्चेच्छादिश्च पुण्यादिश्चेते
पञ्चवर्गा इत्येतेषां पञ्चवर्गाणां धर्मो भूतात्मज्ञानादृते न
विनश्यति । आत्मसंनिधौ नित्यत्वेन प्रतीयमान आत्मो-
पाधिर्यस्तल्लिङ्गं शरीरं हृद्ग्रन्थिरित्युच्यते तत्र यत्प्रकाशते
चैतन्यं स क्षेत्रज्ञ इत्युच्यते ॥२॥

2. When the essence of consciousness which manifests
itself as the three states, is a witness of the states, (but
is) itself devoid of states, positive or negative, and
remains in the state of non-separation and oneness, then
it is spoken of as the Turiya,[1] the fourth. The aggregate
of the six sheaths,[2] which are the products of food, is called
the Annamaya-kosha,[3] alimentary sheath. When the
fourteen kinds of Vāyus[4] beginning with the Prāna, are in
the alimentary sheath, then it is spoken of as the Prānamaya-
kosha, vesture of the vital airs. When the Ātman united

with these two sheaths performs, by means of the four
organs beginning with the mind, the functions of desire,
etc., which have for their objects sound and the rest, then
it (this state) is called the Manomaya-kosha, mental sheath.
When the soul shines being united with these three sheaths,
and cognisant of the differences and non-differences thereof[5]
then it is called the Vijnānamaya-kosha, sheath of intelligence.   When these four sheaths remain in their own cause
which is Knowledge (Brahman), in the same way as the
latent banyan tree remains in the banyan seed, then it is
spoken of as the Ānandamaya-kosha, causal frame of the
Soul.   When it dwells in the body, as the seat[6] of the idea
of pleasure and pain, then it is the Kartā, agent.
The idea of pleasure is that which pertains to wished-for
objects, and the idea of pain is that which pertains to
undesirable objects.   Sound, touch, sight, taste, and smell
are the causes of pleasure and pain.   When the soul,
conforming[7] itself to good and bad actions, has made a link
of the present body (with its past body), and is seen[8]
to be effecting a union, a connection as it were, with
the body not yet received, then it is called the Jiva,
individual soul, on account of its being limited by Upādhis.[9]
The five groups are those beginning with the mind,[10] those
beginning with the Prāna,[11] those beginning with the
Sattva,[12] those beginning with the will,[13] and those beginning with merit.[14] The ego possessing the attributes of these
five groups, does not die out without the knowledge of the
ever-attained Self.   That which, owing to its proximity
to the Self, appears as imperishable and is attributed to
Ātman,[15] is called the Linga-sharira (subtle body), and the
"heart's knot".   The Consciousness which manifests itself
therein is called the Kshetrajna, Knower of the Kshetra[16]
(body).

1   *Turiya*—which is the Absolute, devoid of duality.

2   *The six sheaths*—viz those pertaining to the nerves, bones
marrow, skin, flesh, and blood, which compose all living bodies.

3   *Annamaya-kosha*—The Koshas beginning with the Annamaya,
the grossest of the series, are the vestures (sheaths or cases,) which

make the body enshrining the soul, and as such, are the different
states or forms in which the soul resides.

4   *The fourteen kinds of Vāyus*—called Prāna, Apāna, Vyāna, Udāna
and Samāna ; Nāga, Kurma, Krikara, Devadatta, and Dhananjaya ;
and Vairambhana, Sthānamukhya, Pradyota, and Prakrita. These
different Vāyus or vital airs, are the forces that carry on the different
functions of the body, by directing all the various motions within it, and
are variations of the Prāna. Prāna is not the breath, but that subtle
force or life-principle which causes the motion of the breath.

5   *Thereof*—Pertaining to the desire etc.

6   *Seat etc.*—That is to say, when the self feels that happiness
may be its and not pain, thinking, out of ignorance, the gross and
e subtle body as its attributes.

7   *Conforming etc.*—That is to say, has taken up the present
body on its giving up the last body, as a result of past good and
bad Karma.

8   *Is seen etc.*—That is, acts as if it will continue in another
body on leaving this one.

The word *iva* (as it were), is to be connected with both the
former and the latter part of the sentence, implying that all these ideas
of its possessing and giving up a body, in the past, present, and future,
are, from the the absolute standpoint, untrue to the Ātman.

9   *Limited by Upādhis*—Its imagining that it has a body, and had,
and will get, many bodies is the Ātman's Upādhi which makes
it Jiva.

10   *Mind group*—consisting of mind, Buddhi, Chitta, and Ahamkāra.

11   *Prāna group*—consisting of the five vital airs in the body.

12   *Sattva group*—The Triguna group consisting of Sattva, Rajas,
and Tamas.

13   *Will group*—The Ichchhā group, consisting of will, desire,
resolve, doubt, longing, unbelief, satisfaction, want of satisfaction,
shyness, fear, and imagination.

14   *Merit group*—or the Punya group, consisting of merit, demerit,
knowledge, and Samskāras.

15   *Attributed to Ātman*—Is thought of as Ātman, by its superimposition on the Self.

16   *Kshetra*—Lit. field ; the body is defined as such because
of the fruits of action being produced and reaped in it as in a
field.

ज्ञातृज्ञानज्ञेयानामाविर्भावतिरोभावज्ञाता   स्वयमेव-
माविर्भावतिरोभावहीनः स्वयंज्योतिः स साक्षीत्युच्यते ।

ब्रह्मादिपिपीलिकापर्यन्तं सर्वंप्राणिबुद्धिष्वविशिष्टतयोप-
लभ्यमानः सर्वंप्राणिबुद्धिस्थो यदा तदा कूटस्थ इत्युच्यते ।
कूटस्थाद्युपहितभेदानां स्वरूपलाभहेतुर्भूत्वा मणिगण-
सूत्रमिव सर्वक्षेत्रेष्वनुस्यूतत्वेन यदा प्रकाशत आत्मा
तदाऽन्तर्यामीत्युच्यते । सर्वोपाधिविनिर्मुंक्तः सुवर्णवद्विज्ञान-
घनश्चिन्मात्रस्वरूप आत्मा स्वतन्त्रो यदाऽवभासते तदा
त्वंपदार्थः प्रत्यगात्मेत्युच्यते । सत्यं ज्ञानमनन्तमानन्दं ब्रह्म
सत्यमविनाशि नामदेशकालवस्तुनिमित्तेषु विनश्यत्सु यन्न
विनश्यत्यविनाशि तत्सत्यमित्युच्यते । ज्ञानमित्युत्पत्ति-
विनाशरहितं चैतन्यं ज्ञानमित्यभिधीयते ॥३॥

3. He who is the cogniser of the manifestation[1] and disappearance[2] of the knower, knowledge, and the knowable, but is himself devoid of such manifestation and disappearance, and is self-luminous,[3] is called the Sākshi, Witness. When being perceived in an undifferentiated[4] manner in the intelligence of all beings, from Brahmā (the Creator) down to an ant, it resides in the intelligence of all beings, then it is called the Kutastha.[5] When, standing as the means of realising the real nature of the Kutastha and others, which are differentiations[6] by virtue of possessing limiting adjuncts, the Ātman manifests itself as inter-woven in all bodies, like the thread through a string of jewels, then it is called the Antaryāmin, Internal Ruler. When the Ātman shines forth—absolutely free from all limiting adjuncts, brilliant, as a homogeneous mass of consciousness in its nature of pure Intelligence, independent—then, it is spoken of as the Entity of "Thou"[7] (Tvam), and as the Pratyagātman, Inner-Self. (That which is) Satya (the Reality), Jnāna (Knowledge), Ananta (the Infinite), Ānanda (Bliss), is Brahman. The Reality is the inde-structible ; That which, when name, space, time, substance, and causation are destroyed, dies not,[8] is the indestructible ;

and that is called Satya, the Reality. And Jnāna—that
essence of Intelligence which has no beginning and no end,
spoken of as Jnāna.

1   *Manifestation*—into name and form.

2   *Disappearance*—Merging into the unmanifested state.

3   *Self-luminous*—because of his being unmodified by the above
two states, and having nothing to obstruct his knowledge.

4   *Undifferentiated*—i.e. as pure consciousness.

5   *Kutastha*—Lit. that which resides in the unreal, such as the
intelligence is.

6   *Differentiations etc.*—This implies that any idea of duality, however attenuated it may be as in the case of the Kutastha, is a form
of superimposition on the Self.

7   *The Entity of "Thou"*—i.e. the purified "Thou". Unpurified
"Thou" represents the individual soul, the Jiva with Upādhis.

8   *Dies not*—i.e. remains absolutely changeless in the midst of every
possible cause of change.

अनन्तं नाम मृद्विकारेषु मृदिव सुवर्णविकारेषु
सुवर्णमिव तन्तुकार्येषु तन्तुरिवाव्यक्तादिसृष्टिप्रपञ्चेषु पूर्वं
व्यापकं चैतन्यमनन्तमित्युच्यत आनन्दो नाम सुखचैतन्य-
स्वरूपोऽपरिमितानन्दसमुद्रोऽविशिष्टसुखरूपश्चाऽऽनन्द इत्युच्यत
एतद्वस्तुचतुष्टयं यस्य लक्षणं वस्तुनिमित्तेष्वव्यभिचारि
स तत्पदार्थः परमात्मा परं ब्रह्मेत्युच्यते । त्वंपदार्थ-
दौपाधिकात्तत्पदार्थदौपाधिकाद्विलक्षण आकाशवत्सर्वंगतः
सूक्ष्मः केवलः सत्तामात्रोऽसिपदार्थः स्वयंज्योतिरात्मे-
त्युच्यतेऽतत्पदार्थश्चाऽऽस्मेत्युच्यते । अनादिरन्तवर्तनी प्रमाणा-
प्रमाणसाधारणा न सती नासती न सदसती स्वयम-
विकाराद्विकारहेतौ निरूप्यमाणेऽसती । अनिरूप्यमाणे
सती लक्षणशून्या सा मायेत्युच्यते ॥४॥

4. And Ananta, the Infinite, (remaining in the same manner) as (does) clay in modifications of clay, as gold in modifications of gold, as thread in fabrics of thread, the antecedent,[1] all-pervading[2] Consciousness, that is in all phenomena of creation beginning with the Unmanifested, is called the Infinite. And Ānanda, Bliss—the essence[3] of the consciousness of happiness, the ocean of measureless bliss, and the state of undifferentiated happiness[4] is called Bliss. That, of which the above fourfold nature[5] is an indication,[6] and which is permanent[7] in all space, time, substance, and causation, is called the Entity of "That" (Tat) Paramātman, Supreme Self, and Para-Brahman, or the Highest Brahman. Distinguished from the Entity of "Thou" (when it appears to be) possessed of attributes, as well as from the Entity of "That" (when it appears to be) possessed of attributes, that which is all-pervading like the sky, subtle, whole by itself, pure Existence, the Entity of "Art" (Asi). Self-luminous, is spoken of as the Ātman ; the Entity of "not-That",[8] also is spoken of as Ātman. That which is beginningless, fruitful,[9] open to both proof and disproof, neither real[10] nor unreal,[11] nor real-unreal[12] —non-existent, when, because of the immutability of its own substratum, the cause of change[13] is ascertained;[14] —existent when it is not so ascertained[15]—(thus that) which is undefinable, is called Māyā.

1   *Antecedent*—Existing prior to effects or creation of the universe.

2   *All-pervading*—Pervading the whole of the manifested universe as its essence.

3   *The essence etc.*—which comes only from Jnāna.

4   *Undifferentiated happiness*—The happiness which is not dependent on the senses, such as sight, hearing, touch etc.

5   *Fourfold nature*—viz Reality, Knowledge, Infinity, and Bliss.

6   *An indication*—A faint approach towards expressing the Brahman.

7   *Permanent*—Invariably, present in Its changeless nature.

8   *The Entity of "not-That"*—That which is different from the Entity of "That", by its pertaining to Upādhis. The drift of the whole is to convey the abstract idea. "Thou art That", Tat Tvam Asi, that there is no difference, in reality, between the Ātman and the Paramātman, all the seeming difference being due to Adhyāsa, or

superimposition, of Upādhis or attributes which do not really belong to the Ātman.

9 *Fruitful*—Lit. pregnant. Containing within herself the seeds of action, capable of producing the phenomenal universe.

10 *Neither real*—It has no reality considered apart from Brahman.

11 *Nor unreal*—because it is perceived by all.

12 *Nor real-unreal*—It is not both real and unreal at the same time, but it is something different from Sat (existence) and Asat (non-existence), or in other words, it is inexpressible (लक्षणशून्या).

13 *The cause of change*—Avidyā or nescience.

14 *Is ascertained*—When Māyā is perceived to have the changeless Brahman as its substratum, and consequently when the cause of all modification or change in the phenomenal universe is ascertained in its true aspect, in the state of highest realisation, then Māyā becomes non-existent, as then whatever is, is perceived as One Existence—Brahman only.

15 *Not so ascertained*—When such is not the case it exerts its own powers of illusion and bondage on the unenlightened souls.

इत्यथर्वोपनिषदि सर्वोपनिषत्सारं समाप्तम् ॥

Here ends the Sarvopanishad, as contained in the Atharva-Veda.

BRAHMOPANISHAD

The Brahmopanishad is classed among Upanishads that belong to the Atharva-Veda. From the commentator, Nārāyana, comes a recension of this Upanishad which begins as in the text we have followed. But Shankarā-nanda, who was the head of the Sringeri Math in the 14th century and who has left valuable comments on many of the minor Upanishads, gives us another recension which begins with the number two of our texts. This Upanishad gives a complete and clear idea of the nature of the Ātman which has four states of consciousness and four seats and four places for meditating upon for the better realisation of the Ātman in its Nirguna aspect.

ॐ शौनको ह वै महाशालोऽङ्गिरसं भगवन्तं पिप्पलादमपृच्छत् । दिव्ये ब्रह्मपुरे संप्रतिष्ठिता भवन्ति कथं सृजन्ति कस्यैष महिमा बभूव यो ह्येष महिमा बभूव क एषः ।

1. Om ! Shaunaka, householder[1] of fame, once asked Bhagavān Pippalāda[2] of Angirā's family : In this body, the divine[3] city of Brahman,[4] installed, how do they[5] create? Whose glory does this constitute ? Who is he who became all this glory?

1 *Mahāshāla* : Householder—Lit. having extensive residential hall, i.e., providing in his household maintenance and shelter to many. Compare, Chhāndogya, V. ii.

2 *Bhagavān Pippalāda* : Bhagavān—Lit. means one having the six supreme acquirements : all lordliness, Dharma, fame, all prosperity, wisdom, and renunciation. Of the ten major Upanishads, the Prashnopanishad, comprises the six discourses of this great Rishi Pippalāda given in reply to the six Rishis who came as enquirers, each of whom asked him a question.

3 *Divya*—radically means pertaining to the Shining Ones, the
the Devas, and hence "divine".

4 *Brahmapura*—is a term used in the Upanishads to mean the
human body. One Vedic Mantra (Atharva-Veda, 10.iv.9) seems to
have started this idea, though we find there only the human face
(according to the Nirukta and Brihadāranyaka, II.ii) represented as
the abode of the seven Deva-Rishis. Compare also the use of this
term in the Chhāndogya, VIII. 1, and a parallel idea in Chhāndogya, III. xiii.

5 These creative or manifesting agencies represent the functions
of the organs such as speech etc. The whole question may be stated
plainly as follows : How did the sense-functions come to be installed
in man ? How do they project this sense-world ? Of whom do
they form the manifestation ? What this manifestaion is in reality ?
The Kenopanishad opens with a similar question.

तस्मैं स होवाच ब्रह्माविद्यां वरिष्ठाम् । प्राणो ह्येष आत्मा ।
आत्मनो महिमा बभूव देवानामायुः स देवानां निधन-
मनिधनं दिव्ये ब्रह्मपुरे विरजं निष्कलं शुभ्रमक्षरं यद्ब्रह्म
विभाति स नियच्छति मधुकरराजानं माक्षिकवदिति ।
यथा माक्षीकैकेन तन्तुना जालं विक्षिपति तेनापकर्षति
तथैवैष प्राणो यदा याति संसृष्टमाकृष्य । प्राणदेवतास्ताः
सर्वा नाडच: । सुष्वपे श्येनाकाशवद्यथा खं श्येनमाश्रित्य
याति स्वमालयमेवं सुषुप्तो ब्रूते यथैवैष देवदत्तो यष्टचाऽपि
ताडचमानो नयत्येवमिष्टापूर्तैः शुभाशुभैर्नं लिप्यते । यथा
कुमारो निष्काम आनन्दमुपयाति तथैवैष देवदत्तः स्वप्न
आनन्दमभियाति । वेद एव परं ज्योतिः ज्योतिष्कामो
ज्योतिरानन्दयते । भूयस्तेनैव स्वप्नाय गच्छति जलौका-
वत् । यथा जलौकाऽग्रमग्रं नयत्यात्मानं नयति परं संधय ।
यत्परं नापरं त्यजति स जाग्रदभिधीयते । यथैवैष
कपालाष्टकं संनयति । तमेव स्तन इव लम्बत वेददेव-

योनिः । यत्र जाग्रति शुभाशुभं निरुक्तमस्य देवस्य स
संप्रसारोऽन्तर्यामी खगः कर्कटकः पुष्करः पुरुषः प्राणो
हिंसा परापरं ब्रह्म आत्मा देवता वेदयति । य एवं वेद स
परं ब्रह्म धाम क्षेत्रज्ञमुपैति ॥१॥

1. Unto him (Shaunaka) he (Pippalāda) imparted
the Supreme Wisdom of Brahman : That is Prāna,[1] the
Ātman.[2] He constitutes the glory[3] of the Ātman, the
life of the Devas. He represents both the life and the
death[4] of the Devas. That Brahman who shines within
the divine Brahmapura (or body) as the faultless One,
devoid of manifested effects,[5] self-effulgent, all-pervading,[6]
He (it is who) controls[7] (the Jiva), like a spider[8] controlling
the king of bees. Just as[9] spiders by means of one thread
project and withdraw the web, so also the Prāna, (who)
retires drawing back his creation. Prāna belongs to the
Nādis[10] or subtle nerve-chords as their Devatā or indwelling
deity.[11] One in dreamless sleep[12] goes through that state
to one's own Abode, like a falcon and the sky—just as a
falcon goes (to its nest) borne on the sky. He states :[13]
—Just as this Devadatta (in dreamless sleep) runs not
away even when struck with a stick,[14] even so he does not
also attach himself to good or evil consequences of the
life's ordained activities;[15] just as a child enjoys itself (spon-
taneously) without motive[16] or desiring fruit, even so this
Devadatta (the subject of dreamless sleep) enjoys happiness
in that state. He knows[17] being the Light Supreme.[18] Desiring[19] Light he enjoys the Light. So also he returns by the
same way to the dream-state, like a leech :[20] just as a leech
carries itself on to the other points in front—(first) fixing
upon the next point. And that state which he does not
give up for a next one is called the waking state. (He
carries all these states within himself) just as a (Vedic)
deity bears the eight sacrificial cups[21] simultaneously. It
is from Him that the source of the Vedas and Devas hang
like breasts. In this waking state particularly[22] good and
evil obtain for the shining being (i.e. man's Self) as ordained.

This being or Self is fully self-extended[23] (into world-forms), he is the indwelling controller of things and beings, he is the Bird,[24] the Crab,[25] the Lotus,[26] he is the Purusha,[27] the Prāna, the destroyer,[28] the cause and the effect,[29] the Brahman and the Ātman,[30] he is the Devatā[31] making everything known.[32] Whoever knows all this attains to the transcendent Brahman, the underlying support, the subjective principle.[33]

1 *Prāna*—is generally, but often loosely, translated as "vital breath" ; the "life-force" or the "vital force" would be better. The term is applied both to the transcendental principle, the subtle cause, as well as to its effects, the forces moving to activity the organs, physical and mental. In Prashnopanishad Pippalāda unfolds the whole philosophy of this Prāna.

2 *Atman*—Prāna is here expressly identified with the Ātman, so that there may not be any misconception about the former being limited in meaning only to the manifested aspect of the latter. This manifested aspect, Prāna, is in reality the same as the Ātman, however much distinguished for the sake of intellectual comprehension, that is, for the sake of making out a *process* of manifestation or creation. In the Upanishads, therefore, Prāna is often used as synonymous with Brahman or Ātman. Compare, Brahma-Sutras, I. 23 ; and I. 28-31. This gives a general answer to the questions put ; for all the questions really refer to the Atman.

3 *Prāna*—is here said to be the glory or Mahimā of the Ātman, just as the external developments of the innate genius of a man belong to him as his glory or Mahimā. Still the inapplicability of this word in the case of the Ātman is confessed in Chhāndogya, VI. xiv. This and the former statement in Pippalāda's reply meet the last part of Shaunka's question.

4 *Prāna*—is the life of the Devas, (Indriyas) because the latter embody only its manifested functions which go to make up the macrocosm and the microcosm, the external and the internal world. It is also their death, because their dissolution means nothing but resolution into it.

5 *Nishkala*—means "devoid of Kalās". Now Kalās are the products of the manifesting or creative process. In the sixth discourse of the Prashnopanishad, Pippalāda explains how through the sixteen Kalās Brahman or the Purusha seems to reproduce himself as man and how when these sixteen Kalās merge like rivers in the ocean of the Purusha, only the Akala or Nishkala remains.

6 Akshara may mean the undecaying one, but taking the root to be *ash*, it means the all-pervading one. The term is applied to

Brahman, as well as to Its aspect as the material cause of creation, as in Mundakopanishad, II. 2.

7   Here we have the reply to the first part of Shaunaka's question. This spiritual or transcendental control over organs and elements is fully dealt with in Brihadāranyaka, 7th Brāhmana. Here we have it put collectively by the mention of Jiva.

8   *Like a spider etc.*—This comparison is explained in the next passage. The reference to the king of bees (Madhukararājā) caught in a spider's web implies the idea of the human being with his constituent organs of sense and activity. In Shaunka's question, this human personality is not brought forward, so also in the next passage which develops the comparison.

9   *Just as etc.*—Here also Prāna is to be taken both as the Ātman and as its aspect of being the manifesting principle or prāna proper. The Ātman is here compared to the spider, the Prāna to the single thread let off from the spider, and the complex of organs and elements as the web which the thread inweaves. While Prāna itself is but the Self-projection of the Ātman as Its own principle of manifestation, it is in and through this one Prāna again that sense-functions and sense-products become evolved as well as involved. This is the meaning. It may be pointed out that the human personality (Jiva) is not separately mentioned here, simply because it is nothing but a mere reflection, on the wave of sense-functions, of the reality of the Ātman, and therefore, it is only the wave that practically counts.

10   How is the relation maintained between Prāna and the senses ? Through the Nādis. What is the relation between Prāna and the Nādis ? The Shruti answers it next. The Nādis are the channels developed by Prāna for its manifestation and function, and just as this functioning ranges from the gross to the subtle, so also these channels or chords. The ancient Vedic mind by its introspective method traced the evolution of Prāna from above downwards, and so the results of its analysis are couched in terms which cannot exactly correspond to those used by the modern scientific synthesis which proceeds on generalisation of facts observed by the senses. For example, Sushumnā is the name of the Nādi or channel, as expressed in the terms of Vedic analysis, for the descent of Prāna to the plane of its physiological manifestation, and as scientific synthesis does not yet rise beyond this plane with its sense-observations or material instruments, it is possible to represent only very imperfectly and indirectly the location of this Nādi, and so also in the case of many Nādis.

11   Prāna is the Devatā of the Nādis, because they represent its functions. We have been told in the foregoing texts that Prāna evolves the complex of man's psychophysical activities. The Nādis are here stated to form the media for such evolution as well as for involution. We have therefore the conception of one

Prāna becoming many and then functioning through determinate channels built up with matter—Brahman in its self-manifesting process becoming determined as action and reaction, as Prāna and Ākāsha, force and matter.

12   Sushupti (or as here, *sushvapa*) comes in for a marked attention and analysis in Vedic philosophisings, for in this unique phenomenon, the subject-object consciousness which gives us everything we call real in this life becomes attenuated beyond itself. In such dreamless sleep, this relative consciousness vanishes ; but consciousness in itself does not die, for otherwise there could have been no resurrection for the former.   This fact of potential resolution of ordinary consciousness into absolute consciousness is described as the return of the former to its own abode.   But though this return offers the closest analogy to Samādhi, or actual unification barring even the potentiality for reverting to the illusory relative existence, we must remember that the difference, for purposes other than purely theoretical, counts as much as any other difference. Just as moonlight does not make day, though it *is* the very sunlight that makes it, so the bliss of dreamless sleep is not Samādhi although a little analysis shows that it is the same Supreme Bliss. Here it is the reflecting medium, as it were, of potential reversion, mentioned just now, (or the seed of Avidyā), which makes, this difference. To us, therefore, in dreamless sleep, the Supreme Bliss comes infected with ignorance and impotence; but it is far more recognisable in this form than in those in which it pervades ordinary life. (Compare for this idea of return to Brahman, Chhāndogya, VIII. iii, VI. viii, etc. ; for its deficiency from real self-realisation, Chhāndogya, VIII. xi).

13   How is it known that it goes to its own abode ? Because when one gets up from sleep one makes such statements as "I had good sound sleep", which shows he had been to the abode of Bliss and has returned from there. This Ānanda is Brahman.

14   How can one enjoy Bliss when there are good and evil deeds with their effects ? The Shruti negates the existence of good and evil in the following passage. The law of causation operates on us only so long as we distinguish ourselves as subjects from objects of thought or activity. One in dreamless sleep is not caused to run off by the application of a stick as he fails to objectify the situation. Similarly, being beyond the law of causation, one in dreamless sleep becomes detached from enjoying the fruits of his actions of the wakeful state. Being free from causation, from good and evil, he enjoys Bliss.

15   Literally, "the good and evil belonging to sacrificial and other works prescribed for man in the scriptures".   The *ishtā* comprises all the sacrifices performed for the sake of wordly possessions, other-worldly possessions and progeny, and *purta* comprises works of civic utility, such as planting trees, excavating water-tank, etc., ordained in in the scriptures.

16 If there is no evil, the cause of misery, there can be also no cause of happiness ; then whence is this experience of Bliss ? Anticipating this the Shruti says, though there is no experience of Bliss as is caused, yet there is the eternally existing Bliss itself which is enjoyed. The proof of its existence is direct perception. Without motive, i.e. without setting before itself some end to be pursued through definite means.

17 How can the Bliss be experienced in Sushupti in the absence of knowledge or relative consciousness ? The Shruti says—he knows.

18 Here the enjoyment of dreamless sleep is characterised by a new factor other than Bliss, namely that of Light Supreme. Ordinary consciousness has the threefold aspect of knowing, feeling, and willing. So to describe the supreme state of consciousness in the terms of these aspects, the terms—light, the enjoying of light, the desiring of light—are introduced.

19 How can he, bereft of desires, experience the Bliss ? The Shruti answers that he is desirous of the Jyotis and not altogether desireless.

20 The movement of the leech affords a favourite example in the Upanishadic teaching for the self-transference of consciousness from one object-world to another, as experienced in the transition through death or through the three states of dreamless sleep, dream, and wakefulness. The point emphasised is that each state is complete by itself, no one overlapping the other, so that there is a peculiar one-pointedness in our consciousness when just it enters into any of these states, followed by an unconscious withdrawal from contact with the last state.

21 Just as in particular sacrifices, the libation of butter is offered from eight different cups or pans and the deity invoked accepts them all at once in his undivided individuality though in divided capacity, so the Self supports the three states of consciousness, this dividedness by its transcendent oneness.

22 The prefix *nir* in *nirukta* conveys the sense of "particularly". For the scriptures are seen to speak also of good and evil even in the dream-state of man and prescribe purificatory ceremonies. But really man in his wakeful state whether here on earth or hereafter forms the essential theme of all Vedic ordinances and injunctions. It is man, wide-awake, who projects out of himself and for himself all rules of conduct, all conceptions of rewarding or punishing agents as Devatās, and so on.

23 All plans of existence, gross or subtle, mundane or supra-mundane, consist of the self-extension of man's self-hood. The distinction of the subjective and objective, we must remember, is intellectual and does not therefore operate beyond that limit.

24 *Khaga* is literally "going in the sky", i.e. a bird. The Self in man is "the bird", because it moves in space without any support

other than itself. Consciousness is beyond space and appears to move therein borne on itself. (The idea of time may be taken as included here in that of space).

25 *Karkataka* is literally "the crab". The Self in man is said to be the crab, because, urged by desire, it moves at all angles with the help of its sense-organs.

26 *Pushkara* bears many meanings. But we prefer it to mean "lotus" in keeping with the symbolism of the foregoing words. Man's Self like the lotus blooms in space, time and causation, but draws its sustenance and substance from beyond them. The causal sphere of being is symbolised by waters. It also means pure like the sky.

27 The Purusha is literally one "lying in the abode of body", i.e. the person behind embodied existence, or seen through it as such.

28 *Himsā* literally means "the killing propensity". Man's Self in its aspect of sustaining itself through hunger and food (Brihadāranyaka, I. ii. 3) appears to impersonate the above-named propensity. Or the aspect of self-dissolution, inseparable from self-creation, may seem to impart to self this characteristic of "killing".

29 Parā and Aparā may mean both "the unmanifest or transcendent and the manifest or immanent" or "the cause and effect".

30 Ātmā or Self has been perhaps specifically mentioned here to to bring to clearer view the essential identity of all the substantives variously referred to under the various epithets with the real Self of man.

31 This term Devatā is evidently being used in the texts quite freely. We had it to mean the indwelling deity of a sense-organ or Nādi, and now, twice here, we find it used in the general sense of "the glorious or shining one".

32 Because of its Chetanatva—it being of the nature of Intelligence itself.

33 The reader may be referred here also to the Kshetrajna of of the Gitā (Chap. xiii). In more ancient literature, we meet with this term, as in one Brāhmana, in the sense of subjective knower, "Upadrashtā", as man. But here also this sense of the subjective principle inclines more towards the background of Supreme Self than towards the foreground of embodied existence. In the Gitā Shri Krishna speaks of himself as the one knower-principle of Kshetrajna in all individualised existences. Brihadāranyaka has the well-known text, "No other knower there is except That One."

अथास्य पुरुषस्य चत्वारि स्थानानि भवन्ति नाभि-
हृदयं कण्ठं मूर्धेति । तत्र चतुष्पादं ब्रह्म विभाति । जागरितं

स्वप्नं सुषुप्तं तुरीयमिति । जागरिते ब्रह्मा स्वप्ने विष्णुः
सुषुप्तौ रुद्रस्तुरीयं परमाक्षरं स आदित्यश्च विष्णुश्चेश्वरश्च
स पुरुषः स प्राणः स जीवः सोऽग्निः सेश्वरश्च
जाग्रत्तेषां मध्ये यत्परं ब्रह्म विभाति । स्वयममनस्कम्-
श्रोत्रमपाणिपादं ज्योतिर्विजितं न तत्र लोका न लोका
वेदा न वेदा देवा न देवा यज्ञा न यज्ञा माता न माता
पिता न पिता स्नुषा न स्नुषा चाण्डालो न चाण्डालः
पौल्कसो न पौल्कसः श्रमणो न श्रमणः पशवो न पशव-
स्तापसो न तापस इत्येकमेव परं ब्रह्म विभाति । हृद्याकाशे
तद्विज्ञानमाकाशं तत्सुषिरमाकाशं तद्वेद्यं हृद्याकाशे
यस्मिन्निदं संचरति विचरति यस्मिन्निदं सर्वमोतं प्रोतं ।
सं विभोः प्रजा ज्ञायेरन् । न तत्र देवा ऋषयः पितर
ईशते प्रतिबुद्धः सर्वविदिति ॥२॥

2. Now this Purusha[1] has four seats,[2] the navel,
the heart, the throat, and the head. In these shines
forth the Brahman with four aspects : the state of wakefulness, of dream, of dreamless sleep, and the fourth or
transcendental state. In the wakeful state, He is Brahmā;[3]
in the dreaming state, He is Vishnu;[4] in dreamless sleep
He is Rudra;[5] and the fourth state is the Supreme Indestructible One;[6] and He again[7] is the Sun, the Vishnu,
the Ishvara, He the Purusha, He the Prāna, He the Jiva
or the animate being, He the Fire, the Ishvara, and the
Resplendent ; (yea) that Brahman which is transcendent
shines within all these ! In Itself,[8] It is devoid of mind, of
ears, of hands and feet, of light. There neither are the
worlds existing nor non-existing,[9] neither are the Vedas or
the Devas or the sacrifices existing nor non-existing, neither
is the mother or father or daughter-in-law existing nor

non-existing, neither is Chandāla's son or Pulkasa's son existing nor non-existing, neither is the mendicant existing nor non-existing, so neither all the creatures or the ascetics ; and thus only the One Highest Brahman shines there. Within the recess[10] of the heart is that Ākāsha of consciousness—that with many openings,[11] the aim of knowledge, within the space of the heart—in which all this (universe outside) evolves and moves about, in which all this is warped and woofed[12] (as it were). (Who knows this), knows fully all creation. There the Devas,[13] the Rishis, the Pitris have no control, for being fully awakened, one becomes the knower of all truth.

1 *Purusha*—That is, this central being or entity who as Prāna projects the web of sense-functions and intellectual relations and who proceeds like the leech from one state of consciousness to another.

2 *Four seats etc.*—It is noteworthy that already in some of the Upanishads we find mention made of special centres or seats of consciousness in the body forming stages of spiritual realisation for the process of Yoga or mental concentration. Patanjali speaks of seven planes in the ascent of mind towards perfection in concentration. But specification of centres and nerves in the human body in connection with the process of Yoga had been going on since the the Upanishadic age, till this scheme of localisation matured into the Tāntrika Shatchakra [i.e. the six centres—Mulādhāra (somewhere in sacral plexus), Svādhisthāna (about half-way above the last centre), Manipura (navel), Anāhata (heart), Vishuddha (throat), Ājnā (junction of eyebrows), penetrating beyond which the mind loses itself in the supreme centre of Sahasrāra in the crown of the head]. Here we find only four seats or centres mentioned, of which the navel is substituted by the eye in one of the concluding verses later on. In that verse, the eye is associated with the waking state, the throat with the dreaming state, the heart with the state of dreamless sleep and the head with the fourth or transcendental state. This order of correspondence apparently differs in significance from what we find maintained in the science of mental concentration. But the four states of consciousness are treated here not as they belong to individual man but as they belong to his Universal Self. It is the Purusha in His undifferentiated being who is said to manifest Himself in these four centres, and man has to concentrate on His manifestations in these centres in order to experience the four states of consciousness corresponding to them in all their reality.

3 *Brahmā*—Because in this state the objects of desire become kinetic or actual in the sense of imposing their own law on the desiring agents. Brahmā is, here, the Divinity in man as the creator ;

in our wakeful state, this Divinity *creates*, or has all objects of desire realised, so that the force of desire becomes transmuted into the force inherent in created objects.

4 *Vishnu*—Because in this state the objects of desire are still potential in the sense of being acted upon by the desiring agents instead of being completely free to act upon them ; in other words, the objects of desire are being preserved in this state in view of their being realised as experiences of the wakeful state. This function of preserving them belongs to Vishnu, who is the Divinity in man in its aspect of the Preserver of the creative process.

5 *Rudra*—Because in this state all objects of desire vanish into dissolution, and we have here the Divinity in man manifesting itself as Rudra, the God of dissolution.

6 The Indestructible One or Akshara is the fourth state. It is the Reality beyond all states of consciousness—immutable, undecaying ; and so the term Akshara is appropriate.

7 *He again etc.*—After relating the manifestations of the Purusha in the three planes of consciousness as Rudra, Vishnu, and Brahmā (which manifestations, by the bye, are differently conceived of in later Vedanta philosophy as Virāt in the ordinary gross plane, Hiranyagarbha in the subtle plane and Ishvara in the causal plane), other well-known manifestations within the sphere of Māyā are being enumerated. The name, Ishvara or Lord, has been twice mentioned in this enumeration. (In Shankarānanda's version it is used once). In a Vedic sense, the Sun and Vishnu are synonymous. The term Purusha used here may refer to the Sānkhya conception.

8 *In Itself etc.*—The text here takes us again beyond the plane of manifestation.

9 *There neither etc.*—The mode of expression is peculiar, and amounts to declaring that neither any affirmations nor any negations of the human intellect serve to describe what the state of Brahman is. We even do not express it when we proceed with the negative method of "*Sa eva neti neti ātmā*" (Brihadāranyaka, III. ix. 26) "He is the 'not this not this' Ātman," or when we proceed with the positive method of "*Sarvam khalvidam Brahma*" "All this indeed is Brahman". They are only methods of attaining to that state and not its descriptions. Just as we cannot say of our mind or consciousness that it is extended, that it measures so many feet or so many inches, so neither can we say that it is not extended, seeing that it holds all extension in itself ; just as this consciousness implies another order of reality, to which the units or standards of physical reality do not apply ; so Brahman is the Reality beyond all intellectual relations or standards which give us our Vedas, our gods or our rewards, or give us our domestic relationships and social distinctions. It is clear that these religious functions, domestic relations, and social distinctions do not exist in the state of Brahman ; but neither

can we say that they do not exist there *so long as we have to affirm their existence anywhere.*

10   *Within the recess etc.*—The idea of the Supreme State, realisable within the recess of the heart and having the characteristic of Ākāsha (ether or space) in that it holds the whole universe of evolving and evolved objects, receives ample treatment in Chhāndogya, 8th Prapāthaka. The expression, *Tadvijnānamākāsham,* stands for the *chidākāsha* of more modern literature.

11   *With many openings*—This conception is amplified in Chhāndogya, 3rd Prapāthaka, 13th part. The openings or points of access into the Ākāsha or Supreme state are represented by the gods or objects worship—being, in the texts referred to, the five Prānas.

12   *Is warped and woofed*—That is, supported as threads in a cloth. Both the idea and symbolism occur more explicitly in Brihadāranyaka 3rd   Chap. 8th   Brāhmana.

13   *There the Devas etc.*—The Devas, the Rishis, and the Pitris comprise the threefold objects of Vedic sacrificial worship. But though they have control over the destinies of the Vedic worshipper owing to the limitedness of his desire and knowledge of truth, they have none over one who transcends all desires by his knowledge of the whole truth as in Brahman "by knowing which all things are known".

हृदिस्था देवताः सर्वा हृदि प्राणाः प्रतिष्ठिताः ।
हृदि प्राणश्च ज्योतिश्च त्रिवृत्सूत्रं च यन्महत् ॥
हृदि चैतन्ये तिष्ठति,
         यज्ञोपवीतं   परमं   पवित्रं
         प्रजापतेर्यत्सहजं पुरस्तात् ।
         आयुष्यमग्र्यं प्रतिमुञ्च शुभ्रं
         यज्ञोपवीतं बलमस्तु तेजः ॥

3.   In the heart the Devas[1] live, in the heart the Prānas[2] are installed, in the heart exist the supreme Prāna[3] and Light[4] as also the immanent Cause with threefold constituents[5] and the Mahat[6] principle.

It exists within this heart, that is, in the consciousness.[7] "Put on the sacrificial thread which is supremely sacred, which became manifest of yore with Prajāpati (the first

created Being)Himself, which embodies longevity, eminence
and purity, and may it be strength and puissance to you !"

1   It is better to explain the meaning according to the thirteenth
chapter of the third part of the Chhāndogya Upanishad. The
Devas specifically mentioned there as dwelling within the heart are :
Āditya (the Sun), Chandramā (the Moon), Agni (the Fire), Parjanya
(the Rain), and Vāyu (the Air). The Nirukta makes all the Vedic
Devas combine and coalesce into three, the Sun, the Air, the Fire.   In
Brihadāranyaka,III. ix. 3, the number of Devas is reckoned on various
principles, representing it to be 33, 6, 3, $1\frac{1}{2}$, 1, etc. When the number
is represented as one, the name of that one Deva is Prāna, i.e. the supreme
Prāna which the present Upanishad speaks of from the beginning.

2   The Prānas established in the heart are also specified in
Chhāndogya, III. 13, namely the five well-known Prānas.

3   The word Prāna here refers to the supreme Prāna described
in the beginning of the texts.

4   The Light refers to the same Jyoti or Light mentioned in the
Chhāndogya III. 13. Brahma-Sutra I.i. 24 explains this Light to be
identical with Brahman.

5   *Trivrit-sutram* literally means "the thread with tripartite sections",
and hence the ordinary sacred thread worn on the body. But Sutra
figuratively means the material cause inasmuch as threads constitute
the material cause of a piece of cloth. The cause of creation is said to
be Trivrit or tripartite either because it is (Prakriti) composed of
Sattva, Rajas, and Tamas according to Sānkhya philosophy or
because it is made up of Tejas (the fire principle), Ap (the water
principle), and Anna (the matter principle) according to Vedanta,
as in Chhāndogya VI. 2. 4.

6   The Mahat, as is well known, is one of the twenty-five principles of Sānkhya (Sānkhya-kārikā 3). Vedanta explains it to be
the Cosmic Intelligence holding in itself in subtle essence the whole
gross creation.

7   The argument developed here is : Since we have seen in the
foregoing text that it is in the heart that the real Trivrit-sutra or
tripartite thread exists, we easily understand the real significance of
the Mantra uttered when one is invested in common life with sacrificial holy thread, (this Mantra being then quoted in the text). And
when it is once understood that the sacrificial thread worn outside
the heart is only an external symbol of the real tripartite thread
existing within the heart, we easily realise the true import of the
custom of discarding the external symbol as formulated in the following ordinance about initiation into Sannyāsa.

सशिखं वपनं कृत्वा बहि:सूत्रं त्यजेद्बुधः ।
यदक्षरं परं ब्रह्म तत्सूत्रमिति धारयेत् ॥

The enlightened one should discard the external thread putting it off with the sacred tuft of hair on the head; the Supreme Brahman as the all-pervading[1] one is the thread, and he should put this on.[2]

1 The word *Aksharam* may literally mean either the "undecaying" or the "all-pervading". From some texts of Mundakopanishad, I. 7, II. 1-2, we find the term to signify Brahman in Its aspect of the manifesting principle. Brahman in Itself, of course, transcends this aspect, but as the latter is identical with Prakriti or the material cause which has been spoken of above as the tripartite thread, Brahman, as the Akshara, is specifically mentioned in the present text.

2 To put on the all-pervading Brahman means, of course, "to keep the mind fixed thereon in constant contemplation" and this practice is to supersede that of wearing the sacrificial thread on the body.

सूचनात्सूत्रमित्याहुः सूत्रं नाम परं पदम् ।
तत्सूत्रं विदितं येन स विप्रो वेदपारगः ॥

The Sutra (or thread) is so called because of its having pierced through and started (the process of becoming).[1] This Sutra verily constitutes the Supreme State. By whom this Sutra is known, he is the Vipra (sage), he has reached beyond the Vedas.

1 *Suchanāt etc.*—The word *Sutram* is here being traced to its root *such*, which means both "piercing through" like a needle, and "starting" or "indicating" a fact. The term, therefore, is quite appropriate as used of the material cause of creation.

तेन सर्वमिदं प्रोतं सूत्रे मणिगणा इव ।
तत्सूत्रं धारयेद्योगी योगविततत्त्वदर्शिवान् ॥

By It all this (universe) is transfixed, as a collection of gems is stringed together on a thread. The Yogi who is the knower of all Yogas and the seer of truth should put on this thread.

बहिःसूत्रं त्यजेद्विद्वान्योगमुत्तममास्थितः ।
ब्रह्मभावमयं सूत्रं धारयेद्यः स चेतनः ॥

Established in the state of highest Yoga, the wise one should put off the external thread. One who is really self-conscious must put on the thread constituted by awareness of Brahman.

धारणात्तस्य सूत्रस्य नोच्छिष्टो नाशुचिर्भवेत् ।
सूत्रमन्तर्गतं येषां ज्ञानयज्ञोपवीतिनाम् ॥

On account of wearing this Sutra or thread, they can neither become contaminated nor unclean,[1] those (namely) who have this thread existing within them—those, with this sacrificial thread of knowledge.

1 *Contaminated nor unclean*—The word *Uchchishta* refers to the digestive processes which corrupt the body they build up with accretions, just as the food left on the plate already eaten from is considered contaminated. Besides this, the human body becomes unclean (Ashuchi) by contact with impure things or thoughts.

ते वै सूत्रविदो लोके ते च यज्ञोपवीतिनः ।
ज्ञानशिखिनो ज्ञाननिष्ठा ज्ञानयज्ञोपवीतिनः ॥

They, among men, (really) know the Sutra, they (really) wear the sacrificial thread (on themselves), who are devoted to Jnāna (the highest knowledge), who have this Jnāna for their sacred hair-tuft, this Jnāna for their sacred thread.

ज्ञानमेव परं तेषां पवित्रं ज्ञानमुत्तमम् ।
अग्नेरिव शिखा नान्या यस्य ज्ञानमयी शिखा ॥
स शिखीत्युच्यते विद्वानितरे केशधारिणः ॥

For them Jnāna is the greatest purifier—Jnāna, that is the best[1] as such. Those who have this Jnāna for their tufted hair are as non-different from it as is fire from its flame.[2] This wise one is (really) said to be a Shikhi (or wearer of the tufted hair), while others are mere growers of hair (on the head).

1   The word *Pavitra* means a purifying agent. In the scriptures
we find the highest knowledge characterised as the greatest purifying
agent, as in the Gita : न हि ज्ञानेन सदृशं पवित्रमिह विद्यते ।

2   The flame is also called Shikhā. As the fire is one with its
Shikhā, so the Jnāni is one with his Shikhā of Jnāna. "The
knower of Brahman becomes Brahman Itself."

कर्मण्यधिकृता ये तु वैदिके ब्राह्मणादयः ।
तैः संधार्यमिदं सूत्रं क्रियाङ्गं तद्धि वै स्मृतम् ॥

But those belonging to the three castes (Brāhmanas,
Kshatriyas, and Vaishyas) who have the right of performing
Vedic works have to put on this (i.e. the common) sacred
thread, as surely this thread is ordained to be part of such
works.[1]

1   This verse admits that though the ordinary sacrificial thread
is a mere external symbol that may be discarded by those who put
on real girdle of Jnāna, it cannot be dispensed with in the performance of Vedic works as it is a part of it ; so its putting off presup-
poses the giving up of such works. Compare the Vedic injunction:
तस्माद्यज्ञोपवीत्येवाधीयीत याजयेद्यजेत वा ।

शिखा ज्ञानमयी यस्य उपवीतं च तन्मयम् ।
ब्राह्मण्यं सकलं तस्य इति ब्रह्मविदो विदुः ॥

One who has the Jnāna for his tufted hair, and the
same for his sacred thread, has everything about him
characterised by Brāhmanahood—so know the knowers
of the Vedas ![1]

1   *Knowers of the Vedas*—Here "Brahman" should mean the
Vedas ; for the contention implied here is that those who understand the real spirit of the Vedas recognise a Jnāni, who has even
cast off the Vedic symbol of the three higher castes, as being still a
Brāhmana in a real sense.

इदं यज्ञोपवीतं तु पवित्रं यत्परायणम् ।
स विद्वान्यज्ञोपवीती स्यात्स यज्ञः स च यज्ञवित् ॥

This sacred thread   (of Yajna, i.e. of the all-pervading
Reality) is, again, the purification (itself) and that which

is the end-all (of Vedic works) ; and the wearer of this thread is the wise one—is Yajna himself as well as the knower of Yajna.[1]

1 Here "Yajna", which in its sense of Vedic works justifies the use of a sacred thread, is used four times in its higher sense for the sake of effect.

एको देवः सर्वभूतेषु गूढः सर्वव्यापी सर्वभूतान्तरात्मा ।
कर्माध्यक्षः सर्वभूताधिवासः साक्षी चेता केवलो
निर्गुणश्च ॥

The One Lord (self-effulgent) in all beings remaining hidden, all-pervading and the Self of all beings, controlling and watching over all works (good or bad), living in all creatures and the Witness (i.e. neither the doer of any acts nor the enjoyer), the Supreme Intelligence, the One without a second, having no attributes.[1]

1 Now the texts rise to the theme of that Reality which releases us from the bondage of all codes.

एको मनीषी निष्क्रियाणां बहूनामेकं
सन्तं बहुधा यः करोति ।
तमात्मानं येऽनुपश्यन्ति धीरास्तेषां
शान्तिः शाश्वती नेतरेषाम् ॥

The one Intelligent (active) Being among the many inactive, He who makes the many from what is one— the wise men who find out this Self, theirs is the eternal peace, not of others.

आत्मानमरणिं कृत्वा प्रणवं चोत्तरारणिम् ।
ध्याननिर्मथनाभ्यासाद्देवं पश्येन्निगूढवत् ॥

Having made oneself the Arani,[1] and the Pranava the upper Arani and rubbing them together through the practice of meditation, see the Lord in His hidden reality.

1 *Arani*—A piece of wood of the Shami tree used for kindling the sacred fire by friction.

The analogy is simple in this Mantra : Self-consciousness is the lower wood ; the Pranava, or the syllable Om, is the upper wood ; the process of rubbing is meditation which produces the fire of "the knowledge of Atman". It is called *nigudhavat*, i.e. hidden or unmanifested, because just as prior to the process of rubbing fire is hidden in the wood, so is the Self or the Atman hidden in men.

तिलेषु तैलं दधिनीव सर्पिरापः स्रोतःस्वरणीषु
चाग्निः ।

एवमात्माऽऽत्मनि गृह्यतेऽसौ सत्येनैनं तपसा
योऽनुपश्यति ॥

As is the oil in the sesamum seed, the butter in the curd, water in the flowing waves, and fire in the Shami wood, so is the Ātman in one's self to be discovered by one who searches for It through truth and austere practice.

ऊर्णनाभिर्यथा तन्तून्सृजते संहरत्यपि ।
जाग्रत्स्वप्ने तथा जीवो गच्छत्यागच्छते पुनः ॥

As the spider weaves out the web and again withdraws it, so the Jiva comes out to and goes back again to the wakeful and dreaming states respectively.[1]

1 The text here reverts to the old simile with which the whole discussion in the treatise started.

पद्मकोशप्रतीकाशं सुषिरं चाप्यधोमुखम् ।
हृदयं तद्विजानीयाद्विश्वस्याऽऽयतनं महत् ॥

The heart (i.e. the inner chamber of heart) resembles the calyx of a lotus, full of cavities and also with its face turned downwards. Know that to be the great habitat of the whole universe.[1]

1 Cf. Swami Vivekananda's lectures on Microcosm and Macrocosm in *Jnāna-Yoga*.

नेत्रस्थं जाग्रतं विद्यात्कण्ठे स्वप्नं विनिर्दिशेत् ।
सुषुप्तं हृदयस्थं तु तुरीयं मूर्ध्नि संस्थितम् ॥

Know the wakeful state to have for its centre the
eyes;[1] the dreaming state should be assigned to the throat ;
the state of dreamless sleep is in the heart ; and the transcendental state is in the crown of the head.

1 This assignment of different centres in the body for different
states of consciousness does not tally with the first specification of the
centres as made just after the close of the first text in this Upanishad.
We have already referred to this fact there and have pointed this how
the later yogic psychology developed this theory of the centres more
fully and consistently.

यदात्मा प्रज्ञयाऽऽत्मानं संधत्ते परमात्मनि ।
तेन संध्या ध्यानमेव तस्मात्संध्याभिवन्दनम् ॥

From the fact of an individual holding[1] his self by
means of Prajñā or spiritual understanding in the Supreme
Self, we have what is called Sandhyā and Dhyāna, as also
the worshipping associated with Sandhyā.

1 *Sandhatte* (holds) : Sandhyā (a form of worship in morning,
noon, and evening) and Dhyāna (meditation) are derivatives from
the same root, meaning "to hold", and hence the propriety of the
above definition.

निरोदका ध्यानसंध्या वाक्कायक्लेशवर्जिता ।
संधिनी सर्वभूतानां सा संध्या ह्येकदण्डिनाम् ॥

The Sandhyā by meditation is devoid of any offering
of liquids and so also of any exertion of body and speech ;
it is the unifying principle for all creatures, and this is
really the Sandhyā for Ekadandis.[1]

This and the next verse seek to show how the daily worship
called Sandhy , compulsory for all, becomes transmuted into the
worship of meditation in the case Sannyāsins. The root meaning
of Sandhyā is emphasized to the exclusion of its external form.

This root means "holding together" as Sandhyā is essentially that which holds together or unifies the human self and the Supreme Self.

1 *Ekadandis* are one-staff Sannyāsins, the staff being the symbol of self-control. The triple-staffed Sannyāsins have three sticks tied together, as symbolising control of mind, speech and body. See Paramahamsopanishad Shloka 2, Note 15.

यतो वाचो निवर्तन्ते अप्राप्य मनसा सह ।
आनन्दमेतज्जीवस्य यं ज्ञात्वा मुच्यते बुधः ॥

From which without reaching It, the speech falls back with the mind, that is the transcendental Bliss of this embodied being, knowing which the wise one is released (from all bondage).

The first line of this verse is also to be found in the Taittiriya Upanishad. Some are of opinion that the Brahman in His transcendental aspect is unknown and unknowable and is akin to the Spencerian Absolute. But the real import is that though He is beyond speech and mind, He can be known and realised by going beyond speech and mind.

सर्वव्यापिनमात्मानं क्षीरे सर्पिरिवार्पितम् ।
आत्मविद्यातपोमूलं तद्ब्रह्मोपनिषत्परम् ।
सर्वात्मैकत्वरूपेण तद्ब्रह्मोपनिषत्परमिति ॥

(And this Bliss is verily) the Self which pervades the whole universe, as the butter diffused within the milk.

This is the Brahmopanishad, or the supreme wisdom of Brahman, in the form of a unity of the Ātman of all, founded on the spiritual discipline (Tapas) which is (nothing but) the Vidyā or science of the Ātman.

इत्यथर्ववेदे ब्रह्मोपनिषत्समाप्ता ॥

Here ends the Brahmopanishad belonging to the Atharva-Veda.

ĀRUNEYI UPANISHAD

This is another Upanishad belonging to the Atharva-Veda, and in it are set forth some of the characteristics of the highest class of Sannyāsins (Paramahamsas), the goal being laid down as the realisation of Brahman through perfect renunciation and constant meditation. The Upanishad is cast into the form of a dialogue with a single question to introduce the whole recital in the form of a reply.

ॐ आरुणिः प्रजापतेर्लोकं जगाम तं गत्वोवाच केन भगवन् कर्मण्यशेषतो विसृजानीति तं होवाच प्रजापति-स्तव पुत्रान् भ्रातृन्बन्धवादींश्छिखां यज्ञोपवीतं च यागं च सूत्रं च स्वाध्यायं च भूर्लोकभुवर्लोकस्वर्लोकमहर्लोक-जनलोकतपोलोकसत्यलोकं च । अतलपातालवितल-सुतलरसातलतलातलमहातलं ब्रह्माण्डं च विसर्जयेद्दण्ड-माच्छादनं च परिग्रहेच्छेषं विसृजेच्छेषं विसृजेदिति ॥१॥

1. Om. Aruna's son went to the sphere of Brahmā, the Creator, and reaching there said, "Lord, in what way can I relinquish work altogether ?" Brahmā said to him : You must give up your sons, brothers, friends, and the rest, your hair-tuft and the holy thread, your sacrifices and books regulating them, your scriptures ;[1] must give up the (seven upper) spheres entitled Bhur, Bhuvar, Svar, Mahar, Jana, Tapas, and Satya,[2] and the (seven nether) spheres, viz Atala, Pātāla, Vitala, Sutala, Rasātala, Talātala, and Mahātala,[3] together with the (whole) universe ; and must take on the staff and the scanty clothing of the Sannyāsin; you must renounce everything else, aye, everything else.[4]

1 *Scriptures*—The Karma-kānda or ritualistic portion of the Vedas is meant, not the Upanishads, or the knowledge portion.

2 These seven spheres are enumerated here in the ascending order beginning with the Bhur-loka, which is this earth. Satya-loka is the same as Brahma-loka.

3 These nether spheres have been named promiscuously without regard to their gradation. "Giving up all these spheres" means "giving up the desire to go to these places for enjoyment".

4 The repetition signifies earnestness of appeal.

गृहस्थो ब्रह्मचारी वानप्रस्थो वा लौकिकाग्नीनुदराग्नौ समारोपयेद्गायत्रीं च स्ववाचाग्नौ समारोपयेदुपवीतं भूमावप्सु वा विसृजेत्कुटीचरो ब्रह्मचारी कुटुम्बं विसृजेत्पात्रं विसृजेत्पवित्रं विसृजेद्दण्डांश्च लौकिकाग्नींश्च विसृजेदिति होवाच । अत ऊर्ध्वममन्त्रवदाचरेद्दूर्ध्वगमनं विसृजेत्त्रिसंध्यादौ स्नानमाचरेत्सं ध समाधावात्मन्या-चरेत्सर्वेषु वेदेष्वारण्यकमावर्तयेदुपनिषदमावर्तयेदुपनिषद-मावर्तयेत् ॥२॥

2. The householder, or the Brahmachāri, or the Vānaprashta[1] should commit the fires[2] that lead to the different spheres to the fire that is in the stomach,[3] and consign the sacred Mantra, Gāyatri, to the fire that is in his own speech,[4] should throw the holy thread on the ground or into water. The Kutichara[5] living a Brah-machāri's life should give up his relatives, and discard his begging bowl, and the straining-cloth, should give up his triple staves, and the fires that lead to particular spheres. (So said Prajāpati.) Henceforward he should behave like one who has got no Mantra to repeat, should give up the desire to go to the higher spheres, bathe at the beginning of the three meeting-points of the day, viz morning, noon, and evening, should effect a union with his Ātman through the highest concentration,[6] and from amongst the (whole range of the) Vedas should repeat only

the Āranyakas,' only the Upanishads, aye, nothing but the Upanishads.

Now it is being shown who are entitled to Sannyāsa.

1 *Vānaprastha*—Lit. one who betakes himself to the forest. A married man who in old age retires to forest-life either alone or in company with his partner, if she be living, is called by this name.

2 *The fires etc.*—The Shrutis and Smritis speak of certain fires which, properly tended since boyhood, lead to particular spheres. It was obligatory on every recognised member of the Vedic community, so long as he lived the life of Vedic works, to keep up these fires as the living emblem thereof. The Sannyāsin must give up all such fires uttering the appropriate Mantra, and give himself wholly up to meditation.

3 *The fire in the stomach*—The fire or heat that digests the food we eat. According to Brihadāranyaka Upanishad (V. 9), this digestive heat is the same as Vaishvānara, whom the Brahma-Sutras (I. ii. 24) explain as the Paramātman.

4 Agni or Fire is considered to be the presiding deity of speech.

5 *Kutichara*—or Kutichaka, is the lowest rank of Sannyāsins, the other three being Bahudaka, Hamsa, and Paramahamsa, who are wandering Sannyāsins. The Kutichara is a monk who begs in the house of his son.

6 *Union etc.*—i.e. this union should stand, in his case, for the religious observances which signalise the three conjunctions of the day-time.

7 *The Āranyakas*—Lit. portions used to be read in the forests, hence the Upanishads. The meaning is that the Sannyāsin should try to realise the oneness of Brahman as inculcated in the Upanishads leaving aside the ritualistic portion as having no significance for him.

खल्वहं ब्रह्मसूत्रं सूचनात्सूत्रं ब्रह्म सूत्रमहमेव विद्रां-
स्त्रिवृत्सूत्रं त्यजेद्विद्वान्य एवंवेद संन्यस्तं मया संन्यस्तं
मया संन्यस्तं मयेति त्रिःकृत्वाऽभयं सर्वभूतेभ्यो मत्तः
सर्वं प्रवर्तंते । सखा मा गोपायौजः सखा योऽसीन्द्रस्य
वज्रोऽसीत्यनेन मन्त्रेण कृत्वोर्वं वैणवं दण्डं कौपीनं
परिग्रहेदौषधवदशनमाचरेदौषधवदशनमाचरेद्ब्रह्मचर्यमहिंसां चा-

परिग्रहं च सत्यं च यत्नन हे रक्षतो हे रक्षतो हे   रक्षत
इति ॥३॥

3. Verily I am Brahman, the Sutra ;[1] the Sutra
is Brahman for It originates (the cosmos) ; I myself am the
Sutra because I am a man of realisation—the wise one who
has realised this should give up his triple holy thread.
"I have renounced, I have renounced, I have renounced"[2]
— uttering this thrice he should declare—"From me there
is no fear (in word, thought, or deed) to any being, for
from me everything has proceeded."   Uttering the Mantra
—"Thou art my friend, so protect me (from cows, serpents,
etc.), thou art strength and my friend, in all seen and unseen
danger thou art the Thunder of the Lord of the Universe",
etc.,[3] he should hold up high the bamboo staff and put on
the loin-cloth.   He should take food as if[4] it were medicine,
aye, as if it were medicine.   Carefully guard (oh, ye all
who are concerned) your chastity (in thought, word, and
deed), non-injury, non-acceptance of (superfluous) gifts,
non-thieving,[5] and truthfulness—guard them by all means,
aye, do guard ![6]

1 *Sutra*—Lit. that which originates something. The word
commonly means thread, as it is thread that forming the material
cause of a fabric gives the idea of a new thing being made, which
really is not the case.   So Brahman also appears as this
universe, which in reality is nothing distinct from it. Hence the
term is applied to Brahman also. This negates the difference
between Brahman and the world as it has already negated the
difference between the individual self and Brahman or the Supreme
Self.

2 The repetition is explained thus : Each is repeated before the
Beings of each of the three worlds. It is repeated in higher and
yet higher pitch to tell them that he has renounced everything.
Having thus renounced, any future return to such desires made him
liable to be censured and condemned by the three worlds. Never is
he to entertain such desires again.

3 *The Thunder etc.*—i.e. something which strikes terror into the
the heart of the enemies. The Mantra has been quoted in   part
only.

4 *As if etc.*—i.e. he should eat merely to live, and not hanker
after the delicacies of taste. He is also not to discard it completely

and thus cause injury and harm to his body which would prevent him from attaining the supreme goal. Sannyāsa does not mean that.

5 The omission of this word is to be supplied from the word *cha* in the text.

6 Even at the cost of your lives. Prajāpati repeats it so as to declare it to everybody.

अथातः परमहंसपरिव्राजकानामासनशयनाभ्यां भूमौ ब्रह्मचारिणां मृत्पात्रं वाऽल्बुपात्रं दारुपात्रं वा कामक्रोध- लोभमोहदम्भदर्पासूयाममत्वाहंकारानृतादीनपि त्यजेद्वर्षासु ध्रुवशीलोऽष्टौं मासानेकाकी यतिश्चरेद्द्वावेव वा चरेद्द्वावेव वा चरेत् ॥४॥

4. Now then the duties of the highest class of itinerant monks—the Paramahamsa Parivrājakas (are as follows) : They must sit and lie down[1] on the ground. Those having already taken the vow of chastity etc. should use an earthen bowl or one made of gourd, or a wooden bowl; they should give up lust, anger, avarice, infatuation, ostentation, haughtiness, jealousy, attachment to objects, egotism, falsehood,[2] and the like.[3] The Sannyāsin should stay at one place during the four months[4] of the rainy season, and during the remaining eight months wander alone;[5] or with a single companion, aye, a single companion.[6]

1 *Sit and lie down*—These two words also suggest mindfulness of the Self and taking no thought for sense-objects respectively. For without these, mere giving up of luxuries externally will not entitle him to be a true wandering monk.

2 *Falsehood*—Speaking word unpleasing, harmful, and not provable, and about facts, not seen.

3 *Like*—Excessive joy, sorrow etc.

4 *Four months' etc.*—Beginning from the month of Āshādha (or June-July).

5 Many give rise to quarrels, two spend time in talk ; so the wise should go alone, just as a single bracelet on a maiden's hand which makes no noise nor is liable to be broken.

6 Guru and disciple or disciples of the same Guru or two of similar ideal and turn of mind.

खलु वेदार्थं यो विद्वान्सोपनयनादूर्ध्वं स तानि
प्राग्वा त्यजेत्पितरं पुत्रमग्न्युपवीतं कर्म कलत्रं चान्यदपीह
यतयो भिक्षार्थं ग्रामं प्रविशन्ति । पाणिपात्रमुदरपात्रं वा ।
ॐ हि ॐ हि ॐ हीत्येतदुपनिषदं विन्यसेद्द्विधान्य एवं
वेद । पालाशं बैल्वमौदुम्बरं दण्डमजिनं मेखलां यज्ञोपवीतं
च त्यक्त्वा शूरो य एवं वेद । तद्विष्णोः परमं पदं सदा
पश्यन्ति सूरयः । दिवीव चक्षुराततम् । तद्विप्रासो
विपन्यवो जागृवांसः समिन्धते । विष्णोर्यत्परमं पदमित्येवं
निर्वाणानुशासनं वेदानुशासनं वेदानुशासनमिति ।।५।।

5. Verily one who has realised the (true) import of the Vedas may give up those things (previously enumerated) after the investiture with the holy thread, or he may do so even before that ceremony[1]—(give up) his father, son, his sacrificial fires, and the holy thread, his works, his wife, and all else that he may possess. Sannyāsins enter a village for begging purposes only, with their palms or their stomach as the receptacle for food. Uttering "Om" "Om" "Om", they should mentally place this Mantra, the Upanishad, in the different parts of their body.[2] He who realises the Truth in this manner is really the wise one. He who knows this (and is a Brahmachāri taking on the monastic vow) should give up the staff made of the wood of the Palāsha (Dhak), Bilva (Marmelos), or Audumbara (Fig) trees, his skin and girdle and the holy thread, etc., and thus be a hero. "That supreme state of the all-pervading Deity the sages realise[3] for all time like the eye pervading from one end of the sky to the other."[4] "Sages purged of all impurities like anger etc., who have awakened from the sleep[5] (of ignorance), kindle that Truth (in the

minds of the enquirers), that supreme state of the all-pervading Deity." Such indeed is the injunction of the scriptures leading to liberation—the injunction of the Vedas, aye, of the Vedas.[6]

1 For one full of Vairāgya and knowledge these injunctions as regards the sequence or order of the Āshramas and ceremonies have no hold.

2 *Place this Mantra... body*—according to the instructions of the Guru. In making Nyāsa he may use only this Mantra, the most sacred of all Mantras, and use none other.

3 *Realise*—as their own innermost Self. *Surayah* is literally "the spiritual heroes".

4 *Like the eye etc.*—Just as eyes clearly see the whole bright sky which is unobstructed by limiting objects, so is the Supreme State of Vishnu realised by sages.

5 It is the instructions from such Gurus that produce the knowledge of the Truth in the ignorant.

6 The repetition marks the close of the Upanishad.

इत्यथर्ववेदान्तर्गंतारुणेय्युपनिषत्समाप्ता ॥

Here ends the Āruneyi Upanishad, included in the Atharva-Veda.

KAIVALYOPANISHAD

This is another Upanishad belonging to the Atharva-Veda. The commentator Nārāyaṇa calls it the Brahma-Shatarudriya, i.e. the Shatarudriya which glorifies the unconditioned Brahman as opposed to the Personal God Shiva, who is glorified in the other Shatarudriya which forms a part of the Taittirīya Samhitā. It is at once clear, concise, and poetic, and withal, highly philosophical. All this makes it one of the most valuable among the Minor Upanishads. The story form is an apt device to make the subject easily intelligible as well as to give a pedigree to teachings inculcated. Ashvalāyana was a teacher of the Rig-Veda.

अथाश्वलायनो भगवन्तं परमेष्ठिनमुपसमेत्योवाच—
अधीहि भगवन् ब्रह्मविद्यां वरिष्ठां
सदा सद्भिः सेव्यमानां निगूढाम् ।
ययाऽचिरात् सर्वपापं व्यपोह्य
परात्परं पुरुषं याति विद्वान् ।।१।।

1. Then[1] Ashvalāyana approached the Lord Para-mesthi (Brahmā) and said :

Teach, O Lord, the knowledge of Brahman, the highest, always cultivated by the good, hidden, and by which a wise man drives away instantly all the sins and reaches the Purusha higher than the high.[2]

1 *Then*—That is, after having duly qualified himself, by possessing the fourfold requisites for the highest knowledge.

2 *Higher than the high*—Prakriti, the Mother of all manifestation, is called high. Purusha is higher than Prakriti even.

तस्मै स होवाच पितामहश्च
श्रद्धाभक्तिध्यानयोगादवैहि ।
न कर्मणा न प्रजया धनेन
त्यागेनेंके अमृतत्वमानशुः ॥२॥

2. And to him, the Grandsire (Brahmā)[1] said, "Know
(this) by means of faith,[2] devotion, and meditation. Not
by work,[3] nor by progeny, nor by wealth, but by renunciation,[4] some attained immortality.

1 *The Grandsire (Brahmā)*—A common epithet of the Creator,
who is the father of the Prajāpatis, from whom all beings have
proceeded.

2 *Faith etc.*—As knowledge of Brahman cannot be given through
words, these methods are prescribed.

3 *Work*—Sakāma Karma, or work done with the motive of
gaining sense-gratifications, is meant here, not selfless work, which
helps to remove bondage.

4 *Renunciation*—Just as the three means mentioned above are the
means to Brahman, so also Sannyāsa is a fourth means to Brahman.

परेण नाकं निहितं गुहायां
विभ्राजते यद्यतयो विशन्ति ।
वेदान्तविज्ञानसुनिश्चितार्थाः
संन्यासयोगाद्यतयः शुद्धसत्त्वाः ॥
ते ब्रह्मलोकेषु परान्तकाले
परामृतात्परिमुच्यन्ति सर्वे ॥३॥

3. Higher than heaven, seated in the cave (Buddhi),
that shines, (which) the self-controlled attain —the self-
controlled, who being of pure minds have well ascertained
the Reality,[1] by the knowledge of Vedanta, and through

6A

Sannyāsa or renunciation. In the sphere of Brahmā, at the time of cosmic dissolution,[2] they all get liberated from the highest (apparent) immortality of the manifested universe.

1 *The reality*—which is the identity of the individual self with Brahman.

2 *Cosmic dissolution etc.*—This portion of the stanza speaks of those who through some obstacle or other fail to realise Brahman in this life. They remain in Brahmaloka, and at the time of Pralaya become merged in Brahman along with everything else. Upto this point they can attain to various grades of authority, lasting for durations which from the human standpoint would be very long and would be considered as tantamount to immortality, but which can never be absolute immortality, being connected with the manifested universe. This explains the last two lines in the translation of this stanza. The last four lines in the text are found almost verbatim in the Mundakopanishad, Ch. VI. 6th verse.

विविक्तदेशे च सुखासनस्थः

शुचिः समग्रीवशिरःशरीरः ॥४॥

अत्याश्रमस्थः सकलेन्द्रियाणि

निरुध्य भक्त्या स्वगुरुं प्रणम्य ।

हृत्पुण्डरीकं विरजं विशुद्धं

विचिन्त्य मध्ये विशदं विशोकम् ॥५॥

4-5. In a secluded place, sitting in an easy posture, pure, with a neck, head, and body erect, living in the last of the orders[1] of religious life, having controlled all the senses, saluting his own preceptor with reverence, meditating within the lotus of the heart (on Brahman), untainted, pure, clear, and griefless.

1 *The last of the orders etc.*—The Paramahamsa order of Sannyāsins is meant here.

अचिन्त्यमव्यक्तमनन्तरूपं

शिवं प्रशान्तममृतं ब्रह्मयोनिम् ।

तथाऽऽदिमध्यान्तविहीनमेकं

विभुं चिदानन्दमरूपमद्भुतम् ॥६॥

6. (Who is) unthinkable, unmanifest, of endless forms, the good, the peaceful, Immortal, the origin of the worlds, without beginning, middle, and end, the only one, all-pervading, Consciousness, and Bliss, the formless and the wonderful.

उमासहायं परमेश्वरं प्रभुं
त्रिलोचनं नीलकण्ठं प्रशान्तम् ।
ध्यात्वा मुनिर्गच्छति भूतयोनिं
समस्तसाक्षि तमसः परस्तात् ॥७॥

7. Meditating on the highest Lord, allied to Umā,[1] powerful, three-eyed, blue-necked, and tranquil, the holy man reaches Him who is the source of all, the witness of all and is beyond darkness (i.e. Avidyā).

1 *Allied to Umā*—This and the subsequent epithets of "three-eyed" and "dark-necked" point to the Lord Shiva who is to be meditated upon in His Saguna aspect when the aspirant is incapable of meditating on His Nirguna aspect, as a means to attaining the highest state, Umā-Bhavāni as associated with Shiva as half man and half woman Ardha-nārishvara or, "Umā" may stand for the Brahmavidyā or the knowledge of Brahman, (which protects Shiva from passion, love, etc.) ; "Trilo-chana" may mean, who, as the Turiya, is the eye of the three lower states Vishva, Taijasa, and Prājna, or Virāt, Hiranyagarbha, and Ishvara—for all these shine after Brahman who alone is self-effulgent. "Nila-kantha may likewise be explained thus : Brahman being of the essence of knowledge, darkness or nescience lies subjugated in what may be called only a part of It; in other words, It transcends Avidyā.

स ब्रह्मा स शिवः सेन्द्रः सोऽक्षरः परमः स्वराट् ।
स एव विष्णुः स प्राणः स कालोऽग्निः स चन्द्रमाः ॥८॥

8. He is Brahmā, He is Shiva, He is Indra, He is the Immutable, the Supreme, the Self-luminous, He alone is Vishnu, He is Prāna, He is Time and Fire, He is the Moon.

स एव सर्वं यद्भूतं यच्च भव्यं सनातनम् ।
ज्ञात्वा तं मृत्युमत्येति नान्यः पन्था विमुक्तये ॥९॥

9. He alone is all that was, and all that will be, the Eternal ; knowing Him, one transcends death ; there is no other way to freedom.

All these are the Maheshvara and none else; just as one man alone becomes many in dream so the one deity exists as many.

सर्वभूतस्थमात्मानं सर्वभूतानि चात्मनि ।
सम्पश्यन् ब्रह्म परमं याति नान्येन हेतुना ॥१०॥

10. Seeing the Ātman in all beings, and all beings in the Ātman, one attains the highest Brahman — not by any other means.

The first line in this verse occurs in the Gitā also (VI. 29). The oneness of the Macrocosm and the Microcosm through Samādhi is meant.

आत्मानमरणिं कृत्वा प्रणवं चोत्तरारणिम् ।
ज्ञाननिर्मथनाभ्यासात् पाशं दहति पण्डितः ॥११॥

11. Making the Ātman the (lower) Arani,[1] and OM the upper Arani, by the repeated friction of knowledge, a wise man burns up the bond.

Compare Shvetāshvatara I.14 and Brahmopanishad p.61.

If the knowledge of Brahman is not obtained by the meditation spoken of above, the meditation on the Pranava is prescribed.

1 *Arani*—One of the two pieces of wood used in ancient times for kindling the sacred fire by friction. As by constant friction fire is produced from the Arani, so by constant meditation on the unity of the Jiva and Brahman the fire of realisation is produced, which burns off the bond of nescience and restores the aspirant to his pristine freedom.

स एव मायापरिमोहितात्मा
शरीरमास्थाय करोति सर्वम् ।
स्त्रियन्नपानादिविचित्रभोगैः
स एव जाग्रत्परितृप्तिमेति ॥१२॥

12. With his self thus deluded by Māyā or ignorance, it is he who identifies himself with the body and does all sorts of things. In the waking state it is he (the Jiva) who attains satisfaction[1] through the varied objects of enjoyment, such as women, food, drink, etc.

1 *Satisfaction* : Implying also the opposite, viz pain due to undesirable experiences.

The compound *striyanna* in place of Stryanna is Vedic.

स्वप्ने स जीवः सुखदुःखभोक्ता
स्वमायया कल्पितजीवलोके ।
सुषुप्तिकाले सकले विलीने
तमोऽभिभूतः सुखरूपमेति ॥१३॥

13. In the dream-state that Jiva feels pleasure and pain in a sphere of existence created by his own Māyā or ignorance. During the state of profound sleep, when everything is dissolved (into their causal state), he is overpowered by Tamas or non-manifestation and comes to exist in his form of Bliss.[1]

1 *Ignorance and Bliss*—These are the two characteristics of the experience in the state of Sushupti or profound sleep. This element of ignorance makes this state of Sushupti the opposite pole of Samadhi, the highest illumination. It prevents the Jiva from being conscious of his having attained the state of inherent Bliss. Vide Chhāndogya, VIII. 11.

पुनश्च जन्मान्तरकर्मयोगात्
स एव जीवः स्वर्पिति प्रबुद्धः ।
पुरत्रये क्रीडति यश्च जीव-
स्ततस्तु जातं सकलं विचित्रम् ॥
आधारमानन्दमखण्डबोधं
यस्मँल्लयं याति पुरत्रयं च ॥१४॥

14. Again, through his connection with deeds done in previous births, that very Jiva returns to the dream-state, or the waking state. The being who sports in the three cities (viz the states of wakefulness, dream and profound sleep)—from Him has sprung up all diversity. He is the substratum, the bliss, the indivisible Consciousness, in whom the three cities dissolve themselves.

The Turiya or the Transcendental state is referred to in this Shloka. No distinction is made here between the Jiva and Brahman, which are eternally one, the difference between them being only apparent, due to ignorance.

एतस्माज्जायते प्राणो मनः सर्वेन्द्रियाणि च ।
खं वायुर्ज्योतिरापः पृथिवी विश्वस्य धारिणी ॥१५॥

15. From This spring up Prāna (Vitality), mind, all the organs, sky, air, fire, water and the earth that supports all.[1]

This identical Shloka occurs also in Mundaka, II.3.

1 *Supports all*—that is, sentient and insentient objects.

यत्परं ब्रह्म सर्वात्मा विश्वस्यायतनं महत् ।
सूक्ष्मात्सूक्ष्मतरं नित्यं तत्त्वमेव त्वमेव तत् ॥१६॥

16. That which is the Supreme Brahman, the soul of all, the great support of the universe, subtler than the subtle, and eternal—that is thyself, and thou art That.

जाग्रत्स्वप्नसुषुप्त्यादिप्रपञ्चं यत्प्रकाशते ।
तद्ब्रह्माहमिति ज्ञात्वा सर्वबन्धैः प्रमुच्यते ॥१७॥

17. "That which manifests the phenomena, such as the states of wakefulness, dream and profound sleep, I am that Brahman"—realising thus one is liberated from all bonds.

त्रिषु धामसु यद्भोग्यं भोक्ता भोगश्च यद्भवेत् ।
तेभ्यो विलक्षणः साक्षी चिन्मात्रोऽहं सदाशिवः ॥१८॥

18. What constitute the enjoyable, the enjoyer, and the enjoyment, in the three abodes[1]—different from them all am I, the Witness, the Pure Consciousness, the Eternal Good.

1 *Three abodes*—the "three cities" or states mentioned in Shloka 14.

मय्येव सकलं जातं मयि सर्वं प्रतिष्ठितम् ।
मयि सर्वं लयं याति तद्ब्रह्माद्वयमस्म्यहम् ॥१९॥

19. In me alone is everything born, in me does everything rest, and in me is everything dissolved. I am that Brahman, the secondless.

अणोरणीयानहमेव तद्वन्-
महानहं विश्वमहं विचित्रम् ।
पुरातनोऽहं पुरुषोऽहमीशो
हिरण्मयोऽहं शिवरूपमस्मि ॥२०॥

20. I am minuter than the minute, I am likewise the greatest of all, I am the manifold universe. I am the Ancient One, the Purusha and the Ruler, I am the Effulgent One, and the All-good.

For a similar idea compare Katha, II.20.

अपाणिपादोऽहमचिन्त्यशक्तिः
पश्याम्यचक्षुः स शृणोम्यकर्णः ।
अहं विजानामि विविक्तरूपो
न चास्ति वेत्ता मम चित्सदाऽहम् ॥२१॥

21. Without arms and legs am I,[1] of unthinkable power ; I see without eyes, and I hear without ears. I know all, and am different from all.[2] None can know me. I am always the Intelligence.

1 Compare Shvetāshvatara, III.19-20
2 *All*—Buddhi etc.

वेदैरनेहं रहमेव वेद्यो
वेदान्तकृद्वेदविदेव चाहम् ।
न पुण्यपापे मम नास्ति नाशो
न जन्म देहेन्द्रियबुद्धिरस्ति ॥२२॥

22. I alone am taught in the various Vedas, I am
the revealer of the Vedanta or Upanishads, and I am also
the Knower of the Vedas. For me there is neither merit
nor demerit, I suffer no destruction, I have no birth, nor
any self-identity with the body and the organs.

The first half of the Shloka also occurs almost verbatim in the Gitā,
XV.15.

न भूमिरापो न च वह्निरस्ति
न चानिलो मेऽस्ति न चाम्बरं च ।
एवं विदित्वा परमात्मरूपं
गुहाशयं निष्कलमद्वितीयम् ॥२३॥
समस्तसाक्षि सदसद्विहीनं
प्रयाति शुद्धं परमात्मरूपम् ॥२४॥

23-24. For me there is neither earth, nor water,
nor fire, nor air, nor ether. Thus realising the Paaın
mātman, who lies in the cavity of the heart, who is w-ithout
parts, and without a second, the Witness of all, beysond
both existence and non-existence—one attai the pure
Paramatman Itslf.

इति प्रथमः खण्डः ॥

End of the First Part

यः शतरुद्रीयमधीते सोऽग्निपूतो भवति सुरापाना-
त्पूतो भवति ब्रह्महत्यात्पूतोभवति कृत्याकृत्यात्पूतो भवति
तस्मादविमुक्तमाश्रितो भवति । अत्याश्रमी सर्वदा
सकृद्वा जपेत् ॥

1. He who studies the Shatarudriya,[1] is purified as by the Fires,[2] is purified from the sin of drinking, purified from the sin of killing a Brāhmana, from deeds done knowingly or unawares. Through this he has his refuge in Shiva, the Supreme, Self.[3] One who belongs to the highest order of life[4] should repeat this always or once (a day).

This part prescribes an easier mode of Sādhanā or practice for those who are not adepts in the meditation of the Oneness of Brahman. It is meant for purifying the mind to make it fit for higher meditations.

1 *Shatarudriya*—The hundred Shlokas in praise of Rudra, that form a part of the Yajur-Veda. They are considered very holy and are daily recited by thousands of Hindus as it causes purity of heart and produces Vairāgya. According to the commentator Nārāyana, by Shatarudriya is meant the first part of this Upanishad which he terms as Brahma-Shatarudriya.

2 *Fires*—that is, the sacrificial fires enjoined for daily tending and care by the Shruits and Smritis. They used to form a lifelong companion of every Vedic householder in India ever since his investiture with the holy thread.

3 *Shiva or the Supreme Self*—In this Upanishad, the meditation on Shiva has been recommended in several previous Shlokas, of course regard being had to His Supreme or Nirguna aspect. The word Avimukta in the text, which is a common epithet of Shiva, literally means one never deviating from his inmost essence of oneness, never mixing up with the phantasm of Māyā. Avimukta also means a place in Vārānasi which it is believed is not deserted by Shiva and Pārvati even at the time of Pralaya—hence a place of Bliss.

4 *Highest order of life*—viz Sannyāsa.

अनेन ज्ञानमाप्नोति संसारार्णवनाशनम् ।
तस्मादेवं विदित्वैनं कैवल्यं फलमश्नुते
कैवल्यं फलमश्नुत इति ॥१॥

By means of this, one attains the Knowledge that destroys the ocean of Samsāra or repeated transmigration. Therefore, knowing thus one attains the fruit of Kaivalya or liberation, verily one attains liberation.

इत्यथर्ववेदे कैवल्योपनिषत्समाप्ता ।

Here ends the Kaivalyopanishad included in the Atharva-Veda.